BOOKS BY KENNETH KOCH

POETRY

Sun Out   *2002*
A Possible World   *2002*
New Addresses   *2000*
Straits   *1998*
One Train   *1994*
On the Great Atlantic Rainway, Selected Poems 1950–1988   *1994*
Seasons on Earth   *1987*
On the Edge   *1986*
Selected Poems: 1950–1982   *1985*
Days and Nights   *1982*
The Burning Mystery of Anna in 1951   *1979*
The Duplications   *1977*
The Art of Love   *1975*
The Pleasures of Peace   *1969*
When the Sun Tries to Go On   *1969*
Thank You and Other Poems   *1962*
Permanently   *1961*
Ko, or A Season on Earth   *1960*

FICTION

Hotel Lambosa   *1993*
The Red Robins   *1975*

THEATER

The Gold Standard: A Book of Plays   *1996*
One Thousand Avant-Garde Plays   *1988*
The Red Robins   *1979*
A Change of Hearts   *1973*
Bertha and Other Plays   *1966*

NONFICTION

Sun Out

Sun Out

SELECTED POEMS

1952–1954

Kenneth Koch

ALFRED A. KNOPF   NEW YORK   2004

THIS IS A BORZOI BOOK
PUBLISHED BY ALFRED A. KNOPF

Some of the poems in this collection, some of them in slightly different form, were
previously published in the following works:
"When They Packed Up, We Went" and "Sun Out" in *The Poets of the New York School*
(University of Pennsylvania Graduate School of Fine Arts, 1969). "Poem / 'Sweethearts
from abroad,' " "The Dead Body," "Asunder," "Is Nothing Reserved for Next Year,
Newlyweds on Arbor Day?" "Limits," "Your Fun Is a Snob," and "The Cat's Breakfast" in
Poems from 1952 and 1953 (Los Angeles: Black Sparrow, 1968). "When the Sun Tries to
Go On" in *When the Sun Tries to Go On* (Los Angeles: Black Sparrow Press, 1969). "Your
Fun Is a Snob," "Where Am I Kenneth," "Pericles," "En l'An Trentiesme de Mon Eage,"
and "Guinevere" in *On the Great Atlantic Rainway: Selected Poems 1950–1988* (New York:
Alfred A. Knopf, a division of Random House, Inc., 1994). "Without Kinship" and "The
Merry Stones" in *Bertha and Other Plays* (New York: Grove Press, 1966). "January
Nineteenth" in *Thank You and Other Poems* (New York: Grove Press, 1962). "Highway
Barns" appeared in *Quarterly Review of Literature*. "The Man" appeared in *Shiny*.

Library of Congress Cataloging-in-Publication Data
Koch, Kenneth, 1925–2002.
Sun out : selected poems 1952–1954 / by Kenneth Koch—1st ed.
p. cm.
ISBN 0-375-70999-1 pbk
I. Title
PS3521.O27 A6 2002
811'.54—DC21   2002020534

Published October 19, 2002
First paperback edition, March 12, 2004

In Memory of Frank O'Hara

Contents

A Note on This Book

The poems I wrote between 1952 and 1954 are in such a different style from those I wrote afterwards that they never seemed to fit into my books. One did get into *Thank You*, and I included four or five others in my *Selected Poems* of 1994, but I imagine that there they seem more like early oddities than like something that goes with the rest of the poetry. I think their nature will be clearer in a book of their own.

The social and literary context of these poems was the early fifties New York art and poetry world, at least the part of it that I knew. This included the dramatic, splashy, beautiful paintings of Jane Freilicher and Larry Rivers, and Frank O'Hara's seemingly endless inspiration and John Ashbery's eloquent mysteriousness. We poets and painters hung around a lot together, showed each other our works, and were made by this camaraderie very (or more than otherwise) ambitious, envious, emulous, and, I think, lucky. Everyone had an immediately available audience that had no reason not to be critical or enthusiastic. Also I had just spent a year in France, immersed not only in French poetry but in the French language, which I understood and misunderstood at the same time. Words would have several meanings for me at once. *Blanc (white)* was also *blank* and, in the feminine, *Blanche*, the name of a woman. The pleasure—and the sense of new meanings—I got from this happy confusion was something I wanted to re-create in English.

This double or triple quality of words that I imperfectly understood, along with the repetitions, substitutions, and interruptions that for me seemed to go with it, including the abundant use of quotations and exclamations, once I began to hear them all together, constituted a way of using the language that was very stirring to me and seemed to mean a lot. It gave me a strong sensation of speaking the truth; it seemed what had to be said (at least what had to be said by me). If the general sense it made was somewhat clear to me, its individual subjects were less so. When, much later, I came on it, a statement by Wittgenstein seemed to apply: "There are no subjects in the world. A subject is a limitation of the world." Of course everything, once it is written about, even if it's a wild chaos, is bound eventually to become itself a sort of subject. I wanted to keep my subject up in the air as long as possible. For two years, as long as my close relationship to this language lasted, I had the happy sensation of discovery.

Kenneth Koch
June 2002

Sun Out

Sun Out

Bananas, piers, limericks
I am postures
Over there, I, are
The lakes of delectation
Sea, sea you! Mars and win-
Some buffalo
They thinly raft the plain,
Common do

It ice-floes, hit-and-run drivers,
The mass of the wind.
Is that snow
H-ing at the door? And we
Come in the buckle, a
Vanquished distinguished
Secret festival, relieving flights
Of the black brave ocean.

The Chase—First Day

While stealing samples from the grocery store
We knew the green grass blew, and the cabs attempted—
O close to my heart, white days of some invention,
White didn't you know before?

It was a whale that swam, or a ring in the sink then,
The damp nickel among the white
Rainbows (Williams), white didn't I
Know that the mints were going to check you like persons?

Sleet machines!
I approach you like a moth dizzy with materials,
Dick! disk! public peaces of entertainment!
O lonely place-parking under the wonder-falls!

Did the police bend over the taste of peppermint
With the grace of ballet dancers? do the pumps renew?
White might I see you on the whoming dimway
At day and night, and yet win praise of you,
I'll fold my chair in the summer rain,
                    To Jean White.

Highway Barns, the Children of the Road

Amaryllis, is this paved highway a
Coincidence? There we were
On top of the fuel bin. In the autos
Dusk moved silently, like pine-needle mice.
Often I throw hay upon you,
She said. The painted horse had good news.
Yes, I really miss him, she waves,
She pants. In the dusk bin the fuel reasoned silently.
Amaryllis, is this paved highway a
Coincidence? My ears were glad. Aren't you?
Aren't you healthy in sight of the strawberries,
Which like pine-needle lace fight for dawn fuel?
The white mile was lighted up. We shortened
Our day by two whole tusks. The wind rang.
Where is the elephant graveyard? She missed the pavement.
A load of hay went within speaking distance of the raspberries.
Overture to the tone-deaf evening! I don't see its home.
Prawns fell from that sparkling blue sphere.
The land is coughing, "Joy!" Hey, pavements, you charmers,
When are you going to bring me good news?

No Biography

If followed to Matador
What Spice Islands!
What I-spy lands. Shush the door,
We shall be calm as a print
Seating not revealing. . . .
Is my filing
The disturbance to liberate the equator,
Master Moon? How literary, you
Fire with excitement.
Yes, but I'm a liar for the week.
By Thailand! is this minute livable?
The Bear replies: Here is my paw,
Living while concealing. . . .
He invited him! Who? Why? Oh,
Speak to me beneath the envelope,
Lie now beneath the roses.
Don't you believe it's true,
The unmanageable seam?
What's that? Stifle
Me! but do not let this go! Where?
Love. He follows a photograph.
I wish I'd the moon,
He knows—what? Sees her? Simply. Dreams!
Though refusals could be lively.
Own this, while with a peculiar . . .
No! you're not going to stamp again?
See
Iron coming late. He's not afraid of overturning the tundra.

Ellie Campaigns After a Candidate's Defeat

SHE. Oh let my mirror pay the bunny-tax,
    I'm tired of Shilohs. In from Ping-Pong—?

ELLIE I. I see the sighing spray of spring;
  The grass is jumping, the roots leap
  Phones.

SHE. Man comes carrying a tire.

TOGETHER. We are the willows beneath the bear rug.

SHE. Has any election done less than a wine
  Of beastly furniture? and can we be alone,
  Is iron? when are the maddening
  Steep if consoling fractions of history done

ELLIE I. As when by a sign-featured hand? And she shudders

SHE. I sent these same ladders into pastures.

THE CANDIDATE. The bell of your studio lights
  Drove me to ruin. I ran out into advance
  But they could not turn round my
  Marining out. And I . . .

THREE GIRLS. We are three virgins, scansion-hearted,
  To whom the words of Shakespeare cry our
  Peruvianly-inspired hair . . .

ELLIE I. O matches!
  The invention of the soundtruck can presume
  The natural limits of rights, but sandy parks
  Are strown by bettors, and the unnatural monsoon
  Casts its ballot eternally for oblivion,

SHE.   Say, of dying parks of velvety orange hair,
   Porches to face death's thrills,
   And the agnostic peaches of today.

Rapping Along

Greatness on a day
Meant for steadiness and study halls,
Oh can suicide be so near
And the telephone's valence
Our teacher of reaching hills?
And can the policeman's villa
Ever pelt the other fellow
With the wallet of his stars?

In the reversed dream
Grandmother wore an owl; so that
Silver feet made my desk
A drama: then tiny golden snow
At tears, tears! you know collar
Which the windy tree wore. "O my
Reality!" the calm wind swears
Into that.

Long before I raided the ocean
And the leafage had swum
Away; when the broken Piraeos of a bell
Heavens and force. . . . O specks, and dog
"We brang." So their team bust me
In the will, "Frozen Bars,"
Oh way out beyond the leaving cars
Of stay-you-dogs-in-one-place!

Poem

"Sweethearts from abroad," the madrigal
Sang. When I lay down to sleep
On the team, forest. Future, dear
Elision. Fame said, "She must be Latin."
Within these rooms camels may
Skim a future. Don't shed a tear
My damn darling, on the candle
Which he whom I hate carries. No,
Let him light the niece, sky
And heart picture. Phooey! ice
Below the tram with heaven
In my arms, who cares? a mouse or a dream
Lies waiting upon the divan
For weary to spend its pith
Dreams and calls! the intention
To die asleep, the expansion
Of a moment of inattention
Which an age of plagiarism can never evict----
Oh shame, dear stammered, snow
Where the little clubs are brilliant,
And the fanning park
In lover's track of clacked-up snow;
For mints, your clear summer
And my cold hair! the legs go better.

Pericles

Scene 1

FRIEND
I stop and go, Pericles.

PERICLES
Because we have come to find this land

FRIEND
In the midst of truth,
climates, guitars

PERICLES
This breeze is smaller than my mouth

FRIEND
O Pericles
what is a leader?

PERICLES
How we have grown, dears, since we've been from Greece!

FRIEND
How tall a music

PERICLES
Lies wasting on the shore.

Scene 2

ANOTHER MAN
Here I sit.

Scene 3

A WOMAN
Not that the gnat of smallness itself
has anything to offer the beach
with and through, without our tears

as if some tea had raised a blind
into the concussion of nonsense,
and a coughing death.

In Athens I saw twenty-nine old people
and the sidewalk was faery.
Oh everywhere the rats struck down ribbons,
heaven. A slave ship hides my ears.

O friends
amid the fornication of signposts
I saw a new Greece
arise!

Scene 4

FRIEND

   You know. And yet
   he is bothered by the misery of pebbles
   which hat the lovely show
   in which he dies and does appear.
   He: "Take me back to the faucets
   of truth; my mind is a mass."

PERICLES

   Here is freshness and the shore's timeless teeth!

Scene 5

FRIEND

   There's no midnight mystery
   and no coconuts here to see,
   nothing
   but the ocean's sea
   which will wash history's tattoos from me;
   I hope to live satisfactorily
   like a capon that's struck by a tree
   and does die gladly

bereft, O large, of his sexuality.
Oh as honey fills the bee
while the waves' orchestra's business spree
sticks its night in your head like a country,
and as the madman throws the flea
to music, helplessly,
here always shall I be
and not in idolatry
but yet superfluous as a ski
in a barge; while the withered air
reduces baneful boughs to everywhere.

PERICLES
Good night, the parachutes have gone to sleep.

FRIEND
I stop and go, Pericles.

Scene 6

PERICLES
The air is Chinese!
I felt so strange
the day after tomorrow.
The stops have been removed
and the bottle is filled with leeks.
In the forest a sparring partner
whispers, "We grow."
O maidenhead of today
O maidenhead of yesterday

FRIEND
My lord, I found this face in the sand.

PERICLES
Drop it!

    Help!

    CURTAIN

Epilogue
(Spoken by the conductor of the orchestra)

And would it not have been too late
The gas goes on the gas goes off
And we stood there with pure roots
In silence in violence one two one two
Will you please go through that again
The organ's orgasm and the aspirin tablet's speechless spasm.

The Dead Body

If my entrance is winter,
You won't sunshine the blackboard
And ask the music loins for water—
Oh no, you wouldn't do that!
But if the flowers from outside
Reintegrated the sweet potato,
Then it began to hail,
A cow should lie down in the breezes.
I notice that your harvest
Is bitter. There are lilies
In steerage after the phonograph
Of this afternoon, which is hug me
Tight, ocean! Early in this day they
Met, now it is winter, the sun arcs
Like ruined laundry, a big
Guy, a sweet girl. The moon sings,
"I labeled two entrances beneath her sweater.
And there are two countries for mice.
Fourteen cellars give me cashmere,
Rome, lamplight, and steel.
Now I must go to sleep
Amid the strawberry camps of Morocco."
A stone answered the moon,
Saying, "You certainly make the phone ring
And sheet the town hall
In glorious light, but
Oh, moon, in what rig the trees are
Tonight." There were dancers and
Apples inside the helium observatory
And I again gave my hat
To September's leaning manners—
We sung the flutist, earlier than
The muddy leaves. Explosion happens,
And reminders, the easiest big
World, hobnobbing with the trees
Beside the dam-works. "Hoo hoo hoo,"

Sings the common, "no aviary
Am I." And my knee takes its photograph!
"Life proves nothing,"
Sings the lavatory, imbued with pavements
Of Stonehenges by silences
Which catalogue the rose's. Other playmates ripped out the pictures
And "drave" me my room's orange
To pin. "Open, heaven, their suits
And Chinas, for we are they, now
Especially, among earth's million limes."

Asunder

Where were you when they handed out teeth?
I struck out in a season of baseball
Toward the legend of apples; I filled
The air with the china's whimpering. Duty
Romanced me through the inches of paper baskets
In the Sunday of charmed ceilings. Why won't you
Be kind? Because I am not here for this session.
I am dancing around a joy-filled coroner. The
Ablative case hates me. The hedges are freezing.
You would look nice in a wastebasket.

I came toward my darling last October
With cams and deceiving optional bracelets
Of sleepy light! She received as in bins
My nervous air of smiling as within her hand
Winter's begun! No, for that bitch in violets
Is britches in voices. Animals
Fill the fear, whose benign April will patch
The sea! Far better than ivory clothes!

Now it is Sunday and the leap year is over;
The Polish light is descending a mountain of lawyers
Named cattle, the march is saved
From last Juno ontology. Can the basin reciprocate
African harmony's sleepy films? Negative
Poseidon! O chows. They choose to eat sleepy plates
Of grand opera, times digressing natives,
In clockwork shoes, a medicine to shovel them violets
In the way good counsel cerebrates the scalding shore.

3

He is the comic fantastic
Tents. The bandleaders notice him
Through the saving brine. A dash of fishes
Summers him. He eats chemicals. They
Dash his bronco into the
Sea of soul confusion. The marginalia
Of his lungs!

What social force upon this easy doorstep
Can or may weather his hatless blimp? ·
I know you notice that these airy things
Are dogs.

Who heeds the flying violence
Of his pate, and the medicine
Of jam-filled violets, the traffic lights
Of lips?

When They Packed Up, We Went

1

O candy Frigidaires, eagles, and paint boxes
Paints are not a loan beneath the Frigidaire. No, here's a pin
To wind some felonous hat-dog on; O sleepiness!
The fainting pine needles of racism oppress my box.
Fuss alone at the theater, maleficent fooeys
Of carolizing.

2

And divinely she gets up
And drives down
Into the bitterest theatres
Of leaves and in a frown
Chic races, mighty heart
Of hands into my tray
She sleeps at last
The acres man gives away.

3

O advancing negress of the moon, beer mug;
Heart without its paleness being entirely grown
Facile with inner meanness, casket filled with sloops,
Nut-head, I see there air eyebrows in your gown, Mrs.
Ann Ann Ann Ann Ann Ann Ann. Ann.

4

The hurricane sanctions him to death like the
Striptease of Lenin described by a leak!
Amidst the white blossoms of her first June growing
Down amidst his throbbing bosom with alacrity!
O the ash cans were foaming with crime! the sea
Was bright with your alimony and chivalry!

5

In the sight of your dagger I refused to fight calmly with myself,
    expecting the nurse of disreason to pick me up and throw me off the
    gangway, O specials! Night, a soda.
O faces, facts, nights on, under, there.

6

When the entrails of my really absolute calm
Seem the crying of my helmet, O-may-snow,
Take me to Texas, where the dogies weeping, "Midnight
Hurts your pants, to fight calmly, desiderata,"
Concentrates me on the deafness of "to go."
In Austin the steel diversity is beautiful
As the auctioning of chemistry sets; I nod
And fill the embarrasing night
With these replies, "I shall never go home in a sweater
And the damning first place
While the conscience reigns
In the trench; rats of Boston!"
A kindly white juror is safe as this bench, while
We sleep through town,
And the bargains go up—

O a great entertainer lies strapped to the down.

7

The dads came up from Boston
With violence in their hearing
And their navels labeled
"The people of Venice,"
And they swiftly ate the dabs
Of tootling disgust. Everybody yelled, "Dads
Are secrets!" and "Any boot
In a brain-stir," but the dads went down

Into the city of blue jeans
And calmness. When Death cried,
"Add!" they began to scream,
"Force, Junior!"; yet time is all.
And nobody kissed the dads
Saturday afternoon, Sunday, and
We spit into the endearing carnival,
Seasons and faces. . . .

8

O candy candy alligator charm
This Louisiana chain into the hall
Without a davenport,
But snow!

Atlantis Was Original

Too fanned by so tomorrow's ink knot's weak purple
daisy ignorant fan club. He prowl. Pearl. Mid-
nights. Oh. She is, winking their ("Indians' ") fan club
apart. "It merely tempts me, Jason, my heart—" Bed of New Jersey,
and air ink of their clatter: "Mouses." "Breast." "Show
me into him there when all fan clubs start." Her agrees
finds he him as were went there. "My seams we're
every jersey. Silence. It is a purple knockout.

Because we came here, we did not expect to find perfect seasons
and rats raining, into the tunes of everywhere, by gosh!" Mentality
of a the Greeks' closing sentence. Tam to May, "Borrow!" It isn't.
Mighty. And than blue wests a swings gain neutrality, Oh Hen:
"Art eats waves. Gorillas arch coming. He: 'Widest imbecility
of hardest designs few three Mexico—I'm quiet, singable dodger.' Air is
    blind
but not the paw." He is heaving forward then from arrest's
big lozenge: "House, cool middle waking, drive nits and the turrets!"

The shops are comfortably free, and the licensee's net
is everywhere respected, orange paper packages and meant
speech, frowzily frozen, and beautifully free for the inspectors,
so neighborly, of buildings' China, magic ant! "Brings horse to me
lilac respectability jockey-mentioning, shirtwaisted front nylon
bed nicky intelligence. For each smooth occasion, why are you worried
about the railroads?" She sings in tights to the bed-away, rose,
and devilish fringes— Since action's frail in delightful forge her seat.

Where Am I Kenneth?

I

Nail Kenneth down
For I fear the crying bloomers
Of a gnome race
They come yessing among the trees
Like your Boston survivor
Nail Kenneth down

Pick Kenneth up
For it is necessary that the sun
Will be a comb of the blue trees
And there's no cough to race
The tumbling seething jenny
Pick him up, put him to work

Amid the freed trees. Is this Boston?
Look around you. Am I Kenneth?
"The changing sighs of her disgust,"
A young man said, "am blue-kneed dust."
Kenneth waddled into a store and said,
"Pick me up," and said, "Apples, down."

2

Beyond the costly mountains
Some pills are going to sleep
Frank will cover them with blinding bloomers
Janice appears from multiple nowhere
The sun was a hot disk
How do you spell "dish"?

"The young Ann falls off lie zoom
January ends a room
I am afraid life in a tomb,"
The Doc comes in, "Hi, disk."
"Halo Kenneth, the sunlight is a factory."

Nail Kenneth down
For I fear the shades have gone to sleep
Throw the windows, and hey!
Grace comes, it is a rabbit
A rabbit discovers the triumph's lips
And a tuneless campus is deader than ships

3

With the object of a displaced foot.
Kenneth is reading a novel
Nail us down
Skip the air
The sea is a ship,
And yet a ship of consultation!

So hail the words down, but lead in the air!

(Blue is the air above concentric Lambeth.)

Without Kinship

Scene 1

Somewhere on the lawn of Longfellow's House, in Cambridge, Massachusetts. A nightingale leans over her ironing board.

NIGHTINGALE:
  It is small and white.

IRONING BOARD:
  Over the pill and far away
  I hot a vision of white
  So mental, that where carpets kneel.

NIGHTINGALE:
  Loon, pyramid, shine-shine,
  O bark that has suds, little keel
  In the gemlight, O bibarkcycle—

IRONING BOARD:
  Am I then, lady's head,
  Which you have tied unto a knot?

PEBBLE:
  Kenneth stands for constancy,
  Roommate for regret;
  Our Christian society for clemency
  To the dancing Sundays of seas' frenetic egret.
  Janice stands for Japanese
  Maple trees, which stream about this yard
  As though a mariner'd come here
  To find his ocean hard.

GIRL PEBBLE:
  O Melvin!

PEBBLE:
  Charmian!

(They go together and form a driveway.)

Scene 2

The Nurse.

NURSE:

These modern gems have laziness;
My hat is his. This Denver sun
Shines on and down
What grassy slopes?
Season! here is the soap factory;
There is the charged balloon.
My grandfather at eighty offered
The stanza a million dollars
That could make him feel as though
He were really a lagoon.
His face is now seldom
More than unscientific explanation
For a rug. Oh, carry me, impossible slug!

(She lies down, too, and becomes driveway.)

Scene 3

Roadway, driveway. PATIENCE and HANDY are in their car.

HANDY:

Harrisonville to Spokane
In nine thousand three hundred and sixty-seven
Days, it doesn't seem impossible!

PATIENCE:

A storm moderates me this end.

NIGHTINGALE   *(from below, as she and her ironing board are now part of the driveway):*
Gazing with hope

PEBBLE:
This morning upon the

NURSE:
Foolish capers in the sun

GIRL PEBBLE:
I understood for the last time

IRONING BOARD:
How the fan-shaped crisscrosses,
Which speak to everything, are done.

FOOTBALL   *(comes flying through)*:
I gave, for love, my terrifying heart.
Ah, that laughing, papery summer, when we kissed
The leaves of every down, that showed the field
A prayer, and at evening a park.

HANDY:
Please, Patience, take this green dress!

PATIENCE:
O branches! where is the collie of happiness?

EVERYONE:
Woof! Woof!

Everyone Is Endymion

For the two night of my tea nights
Rattrap shop
Hee, he: mouse, supper, and testament,
Column, laying abstractions,
Lemons, pyramid, algebra, and lids
A metropolitan oafness of labor
Fast adhering to light's zone
Asks you to be within socks on
By Rhone-light, a sea of custom
Landslides, fit and pains
Vastly: land, chiffon peanuts,
Nails, pirate, illness, pier-red parks.
She says, "You got me this way sobbing,
Yet all my finds have friends.
At least you can poach me."
Of constancy her landslide by hats.
Such ones met out with hearts
In my love's town, a kangaroo, an ostrich.

2

The blue beer of disunion
United their leading parts
In sanity, and "I" screamed,
"The housekeeper is wet paints
In cure
Crew," when death-adventurer came,
With bears, Afton, burning parts.

O sables, bedroom
Necklaces, and pinch, safe,
Lorry, billboard, asp, and faculty

Limpets, grass, laymen with coffee:
"Didn't we act stupid without our chairs
In the fashion, this afternoon,
Beneath the tree-bellows of everyone?"

Gypsy Yo-yo

There are ban-dares of "lame" low
Beside "tree" entrance. Hint. Barricades
He ogle. Are the bleeding lifesavers?
Rent hippopotamus! Ave.
Talked savage. In
Says on emp. out
Care, as! bed; free auto tires
Coat, on'd am, O box "e'en" blouse.

In the Ashes of June

I am waking off in the wooded arms apartments
Of cerebrating trees' bison. I think bicycle
No land. And the gypsy
Gives her knees. The sabbath is over. Choir is dog
Am in roses. Gene-harp I love you
Lanes, oh! more modern than Alaska. Entry
Is tree the strewn
Apartment-ships-bicycle.

Music everywhere bench with Betty
On it.
Paris of ragged sighs! Oh love
The boat. Anchorage. Sweetness. Cordwood. And banana
Sin tree sun tea marrying time
Egypt, interest. As in Havana
It as is as, sweet cigars and swift comment.

"Nary a one can go into the coo
Key clock." I live, I limp. She
Is has and does.
And there anything knows
Mutt; they whistle
"Science and basketball." Prey, parcels
When they "have freed" me.
Tonight. Goodbye. A lantern. Straight top hat.

Is Nothing Reserved for Next Year, Newlyweds on Arbor Day?

The rosy future
Is a sled all the furniture
You brought inside
What about the whoopee
Flowers and the chief drops

Slide out the window
The vampire the vacuum cleaner
The pocketbook the rags
The rugs I am smiling dear moustache
You are a Chinese laundry

In a garden of orange snow
Nor mind how far the gables go
Neither the red honesty
Oh the music's children
The gun's original behest

I smashed him
Smashed
The dark and darling flowers grow
Behind the living bells
"A sled is all the furniture"

But isn't cups
Cuckoos and formulas
The very fallen street of nuts?
Yes, here's perfumes
Habeus perfumes! My house!

Once, hound street of doors
They said you threw
Eloping ripeness upon the air
O yes, within my sweater
The rosy future

It ripens like cabs
I hope cigars
The yessing nine of an event
For youthful love the oranges
And furies.

Limits

And the chorus
Of "Wear purple gloves like a sundae"
Circumstances the Afghanistan flowers
The feet under the hue of
The mid-Atlantic,

She has a night simple face,
The accounting for Lambeth,
Lunacies in October,
He wears freezing, he walks writing;
"Your name is Lee

And yet my land
Is on your universe.
Should borrowing expire
And brightness exalt
You would be the campus-horse of sleds,

For whom, as yet, nothing goes on."

2

In the murdersome chorus lines of the snow
An entire bird fell biffing from off a tire;
I see her, old Amy, she puts out the fire
And the trees pull my wings to a celebration
Of almanacs, Rome-air-season, and saids:
"We live at the halt of the universe!"
Are the cups' song; and snowy dignitaries
Fall like laminated paper in wards
I find whims the hospital plate; lingering
To five string, as children-cool eat the climbs
Out Tohu Bohu, for things, in fears, for dogs.
Does anyone hear you smile? Eat the pears and peaches
That Father Ludwig counsels yesterday. Here

Is Firkwild Landing, a notification of stars
On deliberate space, and rational punitive ears
Of a delighted history because I love you.
She was standing beside him in radiance.
He thought, "How can I ever live?" And she,
"The uniform of the gladdest malt is its sureness."

3

Within a tumbling lake you ran brains behind the snow
As though chemise must capture Austria.

To know the symphony of calming death,
O poor weeping oblong!

As if to grow them, the freshness of a wheat
Or holiday dims a granary, the sweet oaf!

Ohio

"Hi, you ant!"
So encouraged unsoaking bees
With fulfillment
Rosy bikes' age telephone if flowers
Havana-smoking wavy tube
In yo-yos' vicinity crush
Ape dash the wintry season.

"Theory were mentioned
Too bag."

Hispania homogenized
For ankle tablets' tall de-honey
(Inseminate!) Havre in crush wander a "Li"
Pore. Climate Junction.
Cow nigh oat sea estranged
Evening high vastness, laid Z,
In "wild pillow," bench-car mints.

No Job at Sarah Lawrence

O woebegone snowflakes, a million cold tablets, alas! merry hat, merry
    commonplace, take place Nan marriage is show business
Parade grounds O peace, winter carriage ocean phenomena eagle rain
Banister. Shy people! Europe dent flake easily Montanas
Sherry. Leaf, O loom! seldom
Beside the Greekish wood
A normless kind sweeping dintless carriage
"Moften" would appear. She peaks
Grapes, lines! Man
Toppled, de oh ho yo ho, canary C-foot forests, at now
Oh, harbour; extra lines
Ring at tea foot and certain cows, Oh the bottom
Of a series! how green, camphor, foot ball, Elmer, sing, elbow, sand
    runners, Mediterranean
Armament of tea!

Long long ago, amid the coastlines' breastline magic
Slantline briefcase's
Sweetheart coop llama and sphinx production
O pagans! hear,
Whore, naturalism, simplicity, seduction, amphitheatre,

January, milkmen, hopelessness, and, stare!
Try idea, it is modern, cigars! If blankets
Mutter in cargo, defrayed chests'
Anagram, O coconuts, jujube, and lingo!

Lady, my jungle.
How fond you are of illness,
Elevation, comedy crash beep hooray
Call "ness," life. Sacrilege
Is gnome silver umpire tam, sin,
Sweet to you! Baden
Baden! Lily petals.
We.
Backed through Tulsa, wintry, China's, freshman

Whose queer remark on everything we noticed
Was "Comedy eagle January meditation forehead."
Weird freshman come true delightful rosy night
Sand jumping Samothrace. O peculiar! language,
Scat, rhumba, trireme, manx, silverware, hoop forget! Bogs
Ladylike as the "perfeeect" hornet! Carpet repairs! Oh!
Save me! logs, "hay-pron," forehead, -sail, oh, of slim

Calcium!

Poem

Roof in me, tone-deaf flail!
Clubfoot, mirror, cacophony!
Orchestra of picture-mail
Seed catalogue of yellow finch-valentines,
Drive mirth to sleep! "Next time."

Four-eyes, November talk-boat!
Swift memory shale questioning
Steep Andes cough tic mentioning
Sabotage quiet pensioning skeet
Buffalo quack nimrod shoots vest key.

O nameplates, foreign till-bow!
Numbers of Crimean Sung
French dog shows' climate speak quietude
Froth Medici Ghent horses, O pock!
Sail me from cart, hooky, and sail!

Sunshine on January 15

"This is my hat's weather."

Opponent disarm firearm
A halo of flowers
Dean London
An apple of early floors
To cope with
Our poor bridge of an
Army of hated flowers,
So goodbye to this environment!

I wish to remember
Their falling fur coats
Whose hair was "too anguished
To limit" the crime wave
Of teased bodies
My loss helps you
Into a hen
And the cheer confabulates once more.

The Kinkaid Subway

O corpse of March! in my ranch
Automobile subtitles. Ranches reply
Ranches apes to angels,
"Ha ha boxes of apes!" Railings
That lift up to the beautiful city
Apes the tree-bout's limitations for
Niceness ankles ankles today
Soon day. O boxed cool breeze! Mex-
Icans! "I love to climb that valley up in hill
To what oh
Peacock slays then cuckoo hat."
But we met on the open street
If Paris, near the breaking of lemons
Riot. A room. "Bake home," sang the wry weather;
"Yes" is what the went-title said.

"Good morning," sang the Swedish substitute, "at last
The title of drinking water is when
The apple of formlessly crying today
Kenneth sunrise." O about! movement
Ship-easing rags! "I clank," sheep-
Hooded then fire methods, oh! Arch
Of banking! "Wade in minutes," she cried—
Ink peroxide-machine May love you
Doughnut, the Kinkaid Subway,
"Goodbye, goodbye." Music. And then snow.
Oh sing! "His shore finally sees
The angry radiator—back lots ink famous!"

Guinevere
or The Death of the Kangaroo

Scene: a street, a plaza.

GUINEVERE:
  O solids!

GIRAFFE   *(moving along the sidewalk):*
  Yes, and you know, last evening there were junctures
  of drunken breath's dear pink flowers on my lariat.
  He put around me. They said, "Denmark and the
  vitrines! nameless one!"

WEISSER ELEFANT   *(crossing the street toward the GIRAFFE at right angles):*
  I remember.

GUINEVERE   *(sings):*
  With soles on her shoes,
  She takes the gyroscope
  Between her fingers,
  And, quietly, it spins.

KANGAROO   *(waiting at point where the paths of the GIRAFFE and WEISSER ELEFANT CROSS):*
  The. Oh the the. The. I gave the pillow a cussing sandwich. America
    said, "A tree." The manager lay dead. Cuff links.

GIRAFFE   *(pausing):*
  Listen, darlings, don't be so sassy. Do you remember when Chicago
    was only fingertips?

ALL   *(sing):*
  Though circumstances may collect our iced man!

MAN   *(who enters):*
  Unpin these benches that you may descry
  The leafs beneath them. Lovers know my voice
  As that which is or was most at the docks

Before they stopped shipping roses to say "*vivre*,"
O macadam. A child sicklier than restaurant
Waits for the marrying blue of a stiff morning.
We seem to go to run about in a stiff roustabout,
Cuter is the pear of string. Common last touch
Is to die at the nest. Roommate, charm bracelet,
Oh I swear, this is Mexico City.

CHIEFTAN:

He is falling toward me like the charm bracelet
I saw laughing out of the window. At this minute a giraffe
Knows the cow who is offering night my atlas.
The wind, curving from Chinese charm bracelet
To charm bracelet, seems to counsel me, "Dollars,
Feenamint, dollars, gun smoke." After one night
With Dolores, I visited the Huguenot people.

CAPTAIN:
Anchors aweigh!

    (The plaza with all its occupants floats away; VENUS rises from the waves.)

VENUS:

Listen. Listen to the bouquet.
Baby, that placing powder in the pistols,
Married, and placing pistols in the bouquet,
Left me to be long ago at this moment,
Lively the goddess, a headache. A market
Of fleas!

    (It is Paris, a Place. VENUS disappears.)

FIRST FLEA:
Let go of my left elbow.

SECOND FLEA:
That's your potbelly!

A PINK GIRL:
I chanced to find these two
Arguing. There were sadly smoke,
Giant cow-guns, shoguns; and, it appears,
A glass page blonder as a neck of blue jeers.

GIRAFFE AND VENUS   (entering together):
Aren't we a stray couple
From No Land? Oh when
Will catching diseases fly in our plane?

PILOT:
Never! Take everyone a box.

(He passes out little boxes, which, when they are opened, reveal white pieces of paper.)

WEISSER ELEFANT   (reads):
"The bench you are sitting on is made of orange boa
constrictors which have been treated with piratical
chocolate Georgia-bannisters. The Maryland of your
face. Despite what you have been, ho ho, the incine-
rator is not a call girl. Depart before the ice cream
melts." Mine is about food!

GUINEVERE   (throwing herself on Weisser Elefant):
O my lover, my lover!

PILOT:
Wait a minute. Read yours.

GUINEVERE   (gazes into VENUS'S face):
"Your head may be paralyzed by lint." Orchids! buzz saws!

44

ORCHIDS:
This is not blood. This is an orchard
Through which you may walk. Like a bug.

BUZZ SAW:
Everybody: one, two, three!
Plywood!
Goldsmith!
Sunglasses!

(The plaza splits in two like an orange. WEISSER ELEFANT eats half of it. On the other half, Guinevere is playing a guitar to the KANGAROO, and playing cards are falling from his pocket. In the slight breeze one can just make out the chorus of neckties. It seems as if the Old World has become the New. A MOUSE enjoys this séance.)

MOUSE:
God plays the guitar
And Religion listens.
The weary squash
Lurks beside the lotus.
See! the glass buildings
Decide nothing.
We are the sobbing world,
Just as they are in the nude.

GUINEVERE   *(very loud):*
Photomatic bad living
Gigantic prisms. Beaued. Gee. Leaves!

KANGAROO   *(softly):*
Pretty Geneva, pretty Southland, beloved orchestra!

GUINEVERE:
I am pink in the nude.

KANGAROO:
   Yes yes.

GUINEVERE:
   O Joy!

KANGAROO:
   Listen. Baccalaureate. Is that
   Prometheus?

MAN   *(wearing a large mouse head and playing the guitar):*
   Only in the bathroom, knees would care
   And the table of good red air
   Seriously affronts the car
   With the yellow daffodils of today.
   Somnolent I see an amethyst
   Clearing the way for future
   Eons, the ragged hoop
   And the dippy Fragonard of fluffier days,
   Played to the tune of our pablum violin.

GUINEVERE   *(throws herself, kissing, against a statue):*
   O you, concede that I am the airport!

MAN WITH MOUSE HEAD:
   America is like an elephant whose baseballs
   Are boundaries
   Of sunlight. This is peppermint,
   That billiard shore. Now she gets,
   Like horror, the main idea, a stove that is
   Brilliant as the curling raspberries and move to his heart.
   O olives, I know your reputation for fairness,
   And every pipe dreams of a shirtwaisted kimono
   Beyond the callow limousine of the funnies; but Nugent
   Drank the Coca-Cola, and Allen left the boudoir
   Where Jane lay down like a saint, the music of a thumb

Daring the elate, childless strings.
O mothers, weevil, marketplace of the Sixties,
What is the road to Gary, China?

GUINEVERE:
Should industry delay,
Or mice parade? Is that a youth group
Singing: "Daft, weird, kind pennons,
Yo-yos and hills, shirts and displays"?

MAN WITH MOUSE HEAD:
O Germany of sofas,
Are we so clear
As beer is harmless?

GIRAFFE:
A shoplifting land of railroad pyjamas
Passed my door, evil film stars.
Huguenot! evil girls of film-star plantation!

HIPPO:
Yes because we meant to spend the summer;
But now we see the human element
Is merely a white bear, tipping stars
By the briefcase of a violet hand
Meant to inform and believe concatenated
The surface of a wheel-lake or *morgen*
Meaning *morning* in German. Yes I meant
To thumb a ride along the Champs Elysées,
But the sunny Negro
Of handsome stars
Bid for the fingers of my door, and lo! I lay,
The Hippopotamus, sweating as if funny
Water may come true even in the summertime
And—

(Bang! The HIPPO falls dead.)

SOMEONE:
Pure Pins the Lobster!

(YELLOWMAY comes in and takes off all Guinevere's clothes;
GUINEVERE puts her clothes back on.)

GUINEVERE:
The shortest way to go home yesterday
He always called the best way.
There's no suffering in a limeade
Of clearer captains, carpenters, and shipwrights
From grains solidly
In the pier. Oh the white shore, the red sea—

(YELLOWMAY takes her hand; they walk along the seashore.)

YELLOWMAY:
And the works of pineapple.
I have often been a shipmaster
But never a ship. The blow from Tangiers
Never came.

GUINEVERE:
Soldiers waiting at my hammock
Counseled me, "Be as back as soot."
Oh nuts, the chairs have gone away.

YELLOWMAY:
Paintings of the sea, I won't reveal to you my name is Yellowmay.

MAN   (without the mouse head):
Or the lobster
That oval
Which I often noticed.
I think,
"Is this a cigar

48

Or, baby! maybe
The license for a white cigarette,
Given by the shields."
And when the frog becomes a bicycle,
Dear days of pineapple,
Lilac where the giant ripple
Rushes, as past a kangaroo.

KANGAROO:
O mournful existence within a matchbox
With a sullen cockatoo
Whose brain beats its own division
And dandy "wawa"—

OCEAN:
Oh Sweden is endless! the earliest time to drink.

YELLOWMAY:
Are we drinking in chairs like a column?

GUINEVERE:
Oh yes, master. Come jinx with the merry columbine!

(Suddenly it is spring. The HIPPO appears solus, covered with garlands of flowers.)

HIPPO:
Decency of printemps O
Knocks on my pillow!
Houses without a door!
Suitcases which miss my sleeves!
O bears, you, too, on the misty shore
Of the sea, in whose elbows
I hear a moth beginning
To mourn on a blue, beautiful violin.

(The SKY descends, covering all with blue; from the empty stage comes a song.)

  Who cares about them
  In a grouping again
  Or the poking amethyst
  And delicious anthem?
  The bread in the butter box
  And a dictionary—
  The day fears to tell me
  Of white screams. Oh, don't you know it,
  The marriage of blue-
  Bells, America, generous, as white screens
  Failing, the magazine basement
  Of archways. Water
  The generous magazines!

  Summery blue daylight
  The manner of machines,
  Daguerrotype, cigarette store.

  (The dead body of the KANGAROO is dragged across the stage by a two-horse cart.)

The Cat's Breakfast

Air-front days

O cardinal the red robes of an angel
Are falling off the winter too
In the season of are we I ate fist
True hail! the sigh's blue
Wheat, wheat
Whose clothes are stationed mines
A lost canals of love

Through reading dance
But where the event's lust
Did not begin quietly, does
Answer on my toes
Winter, weights, seepy ties

Writer, sandbaggery, troths
Freeze the painter
Hams' collectives'
Summers' tunes' qualities

As we are. Nights.
Heat hums, "Airway the madman
Comes: 'too,' " so wish we advance.

Your Fun Is a Snob

Amnesty store by the facing machine
In the winter of glove
Raiding Western minutes
She spoke low, as a dram,
"On the hinge of a dainty glue
Hundred daisy become a fox
Listen, to what these pinstripes bore
A sin from firewood, up this day
Stump, wheat, end! at my mule team passes
In with love Death Valley."
Through, goodbye mainland!
"These tears, I'm stacking way,"
She whirling smiled, "goodbye," is the plan
Of aspen rain-tinned sunlight, on, "ahem!"

In the next minute the feature is oh
I am backing, science
Halve the apple, plates, come, too.
She is reading in her silk stocking,
La la: "I've got a famous apartment
In cooking. Religion
In the worst ways, that leaves to the basement,
What I know
The handmade height is made you
Is fun, but your fun is a snob."
Agrees, to walk out, illness, the wax taxis,
Reading, "Hopeless mints of lead. . . ." So her
Shy lends night, a helpless manner
Without, in leaflets, to within, often "we're," the crib.

The Merry Stones

Scene 1

A room in a house by the sea. Roy, a young man, is lying in bed. Ingelil, a young Swedish nurse, is standing at the bedside.

INGELIL:

Lay down and be slumbering. A cabinet is kind. The
music is full of fishes. Have some liberty. Eat colds.
Don't be neglected. Board up the hose. Thank the rip-
tides. Lose collectedness. Break, break the ramps.

ROY:

I went to smiling wrists.

INGELIL:

Govern the deciding wasps. Age new badness. Sign
Lohengrin. Be out on the Caspian.

ROY:

Locks were coming in bananas.
Furniture is necks.
Sacrilege is leaning on tiny horse.
A lamprey, oh, has begun to kiss
The sea.

INGELIL:

Use the deigning colors of this cabinet for your windows; only don't,
when the winter comes, complain of the cannon-fare of the horses; for
as surely as hay is tucked into the orphan straw, time will have guess his
last lust in the ephemeral killing bottle. I am a laziness that comes from
a nuttier country; I see to not understand your flailing indecrepitude.
May the blue star of yesterday pink its liberal summit to that head, this
yours, which, like a revolvement, fats the walls with lowing
circumvention. Oh, goodbye, normal!

ROY:

Farewell, moral, and may the neckerchiefs of humming be kind cousins to your gloom. The illiterate flowers are incompatible with shows.

Scene 2

A room. JIM, a young man, is lying in bed.

JIM:

If I should die, myself,
Give me the wallpaper
And wrap me up around the ceiling,
As if sky to an ornament.
Oh how fitting is my known
Beneath the dense whack of the sheet;

If mattress covers in truth
Were known, ah, steel would be riven!
But I am back to my back
On flowers, like the Chinese river
Sink-you-and-go-long-go-she-go,
And music is everywhere.
I wonder if this knife
Would not slay me like an imbecile
If I let it fall, down snow-light
In registered rocks from here—

(He seems to stab himself.)

Oh, lie steep as a swan!
Exaggeration of comments, then help me!

Scene 3

A bare stage.

MASTER OF CEREMONIES   *(about forty-five years old):*
Here are the starriest chain-waving starvers
That ever an eyeball sees, O chasing frankness with sleds!

(Exit M.C.)

FIRST SHOWGIRL:
   I am the music bell of doughnuts, ruthful ball,
   Beds at night in the Sierras, the beach of brass
   That an annoyedly soft breast dims,
   And my revealing counsels are foolish with sonnets.

SECOND SHOWGIRL:
   The least of time's molluscs, and last of the golden hinters
   Am I, come down to Seventieth with my scants on!
   I am teas
   Without formulas! London!

THIRD SHOWGIRL:
   I am the bashful banditress of beans,
   Irritants, Coca-Cola, and steaks.
   I lie beyond the built-in Sierra of plates
   To see our cares mated to a roach in oblivion!

MASTER OF CEREMONIES   *(reenters; he is much younger):*
   So seize your hats,
   Be merry as a phone,
   And cry out at the graying night,
   "Oh thou high pajama of happiness!"
   Last week
   I felt it know you care so cold.

Scene 4

In the Sierras.

ELDERLY MAN:
   A season is my birthright; for which reason
   Winter is very indebted to hats. We are
   Condemning you to
   Breath under water.

BOB:

But I am a mountain lad! my whole bearing and being
Calls out for freedom from Fordham.

ELDERLY MAN:

Nevertheless, go under;
And when you rise, the flowers of heat
Will open your eyes,
And you shall see this Sierra
As the beautiful door to the bust
Of the highly chlorinate female wind
Who hides the masculine hills in her boxes;
The magic of forceful steam
Will be yours, and the shying parts of airplanes,
The linked romance of degustation
And paralysis, to lie on, in the nights of tragic green.

BOB:

I am asea with lust!

ELDERLY MAN:

Yet no more forgotten
Than a cast-iron ring.
We are bored by the midday of flowers,
The Romeo riling amid the wildflowers,
And the beggar the boar smiling into the flowers.

Scene 5

A hotel room.

AL   *(a young husband):*
There is another scene than this hotel room!
Where the boy tries to take his life!
O monsters, my wife!

NELLIE *(his wife):*
He is walking the floor in rings!
I once saw a Swedish stand amid the flowers and throw blood upon
dancers, while sick man, roving up on the bourgeoisie, held in his
hats the swan of their hands, as though a telephone rings.
(Ring. It is a doorbell. Enter BOB.)

NELLIE *(Throws her arms around AL):*
Did you send for the bugles of Lancaster?

The Days to Solve

1

There are empty cars of an absolute beauty
Waiting for me beneath the dress
Of day. The lion has shaved,
And hell is willing,
O affair O affair!

Acting summer removes the disk
Of lilac stupidity.
There are sharp reeds in the city
For disintegration.
I watch a love fall. Hills!

2

Master Chicago! oh the sunlight in milk
Of parenthood! When vichy threw out
Its arrival to blossom saint
And froze the radios like backs
Of cigarette-bards,
Champagne-leaves, Pepper Martin
And true-loves, auto gypsy
Of the ceiling-sink to the Rome we cut
In starlight, delicately alone
Like flag-boys, meeting after sound
Had turned the head blue!

3

May the gross air be
Sonnet! O bigness!
Grape ships!

Den of mines, use,

There is not a taint on her foot
Made by an it or a madman
Often flowers and shoes' remedy—
Million. Foe in act's hire!

The bread is beautiful beneath the sunlight
Easily medley deep at silence
Sews. As the air is right
By hit's orange graph.

January Nineteenth

Houses do not fail to sing in a ghostly way among themselves.
"I felt foolish in the fish market of white horses." "She hands me the
    pleasant nucleus."
"The French parliament have grouped themselves around silence." Yes,
    the houses sing!
"The ear sails itself into the wintry custom of door telephones!" Wintry
    lake!
Bassinets leak through the covers of ice-dripping magazines
Of Clark Bar kindness, in the midst of Romeo My Telegraph Street. Like
    a wheel of cigars
Unfinished by Perseus, the coconut bra parts with chilblains
The unbanished sidewalk, where secret members of the Tear walk. O
    boisterousness!
"She wears a tiara of idleness, she has cocoa on her chair-bonnet;
Each of her children is worth sixteen dollars a million, her hat is in
    Nebraska;
Her feet are in South Fort Worth, Texas, and the ale manufacturers
Are agreed to cut crisscrosses in green upon the lilac statue of her
    milliner—"
So—"my strength!"
"The cheerleaders have penciled the bathtubs with the words 'Maine
    State'
So as not to be bothered by her prettiness, her booths have become a
    sidewalk, her eyes a dove
On the cover of Plinth magazine, and her groceries the weather
In red and green; the weather is costly and marvelous!" The shoe slips,
    and the eye comes, off,
But the basket of circuses is still free on the arm of the sanctified circus
    deliverer,
Whose swift speeches cancel our leaves for seventy weeks. "Bakery of
    coffee gloves!
Oh Lorna Doone fizzled the dazzling icicle-pencil
By sheer blue shirts." My hill! "Let's turn to the pathway of potatoes!"

2

Buttes-Chaumont pleased Aragon; the fire department say, "Flint is our
religion."
The bone Andes are still pledging facial Switzerland to Peruvian
intestinal prisms
Too coffeelike to replace the face; but then that tissue paper is their
business. Our replica
Of all this is the sunset, a basilica of friendly brassieres—
The government of Switzerland may not be overcome by gonorrhea!
Finland wants "boats." The sheep want to go to Finland.
"Sand will not make you a very thrilling overcoat," the house said to me;
Our peach tree sat down. "Chalk was dreaming of the lightning and
thunder."

The hilt of the swords! the hilt of the swords!
The sheep tree, the lightning and thunder!
Powder writes another novel to itself:
Passengers, adroit pyramids, and blue triremes!
Oh how I hate to "Gogol"! Now, baby sweater!
The Green Cab Sighs have fallen in love.

En l'An Trentiesme de Mon Eage

O red-hot cupboards and burning pavements, alas it's summer my cheeks
    fall into somewhere and alas for the Rainbow Club.
Flowery pins bluejay introspection anagrams. On this day I complete my
    twenty-ninth year! I remember the lovely margarine
And the ack-ack of the Chinese discomfortable antiaircraft bullets
    shouting into the clay weather like a beachball in *Terry and the Priates*,
A canoe in shorts, or a laughing raincoat of Bessemer steel. What
    lightness it is to be still
Here, among the orange living, like a spine faculty in the harvest
    diversity cup, a red Chinese giraffe that imitates a rose
Like a lover of steel mittens in collarbone harness time, blimp-lovely, and
    hooky players in the green shark
Museum, the sand everywhere around, forming a coat for the naked
    pencils; the last laugh is on me, says air—
O spring! no, summer! O winter!

The coconut magistrate adopted my little sister, "Cousin."
She had always wear a green sweater and toy play in the sybaritic air.
I am trying to clean up the loft, I can do it a lot easier, with blue air
And red seagulls and green crashes. "Cousin" was put among the simple
    cases,
And when she came to see me (that was during my sixteenth summer), I
    said,
Cousin are you glad to be home? and she handed me a lime swimmer.
Boys often ask me my advice on how they can become more sensitive
To orange wagons sunning themselves beside green curbstones, but
    "Cousin" said,
Take this lime advance. Shoe box. We are swimming toward a coffee
    aspirin tablet.
I didn't know what it meant at the time; and when "Cousin" was packed
    away
With the other Christmas ornaments, she asked me once more,
    California lime Swinburne?
But Mother and I laughed at her little cookies and went home. What
    does it mean?
"Chorusgirl" was the name of a dog I had aged seven. I kept him until I

was nineteen. In nineteen forty-four he reappeared as an ancient cook.
    But one could see the laughing young eyes beneath her (his) gray hair.
And then I touched Coffee Silverware in the Park on her lime-colored
    shoulder, and we kissed
After eating close to a million hamburgers, and drinking bourbon out of
    little hollow glass trees.
That was the advantage of living close to Kentucky! The sedge
    laboratories closed down over New Year's
Day, so Kent and I had to search the barnyard for a light blue accident
Machine; he went to Texas in the same year and founded a shortage
    hospital
Of pure ice, toward which lovely secret purple ladders fell. I sandwiched
In seeing him while I was canoeing through there in the army. Our
Regimental insignia was an ordinary, clean polar bear looking at the sun
As if he were surprised to be in a war. . . . To not hear coconut music
Was all right, but once I did . . . ! O dreams! O nostalgia! A campus of
    cotton roses to detach my wristwatch
Was my dream, and matchsticks the color of yellow real estate, with
    white bearskin gloves
To hold a pink apple! It took place on a bed in New York, a rich
    neighborhood, O coffee-covered sentimentality!

What is your knowledge of the novel? is it happy? are you trying to cover
    up for the green ants? When will the popcorn graduate? The peach's
    mother and father came down to the wedding in fuzz.
Grasping for the boat rail, I inquired after "Cousin" and was showered
    with green lemons. I didn't know you were in love with her! I said to
    Raspberry Corpuscle. He shoved me out into the water.
Amid this blue clothing was I dying or living? how old was I? I had not
    yet published "Fuel Bedrooms," so let me see. . . . Nancy's hands were
    covered with glass sandwiches. She offered me seventeen. I said,
    They're green! She said, Gondolier!
The towers fell down. Mr. Howard, Mrs. Raspberry. Rosemary
    Character Study was holding the candy door wide open for me. . . .
Clean up the happy boats, my son, for we're going to take a vacation
    manuscript. Doctor "Raspberries" to tell me I'm crazy still in the

future like a white plywood
Airplane. But Jane bought paints! We fractured the coffin-balloon. She
    wore a redbird hat. Alice favored the Cubs. Together they fought with
    tinfoil spoons. A glass of beer-water please!

September. The red photograph-milkmen's clay hods
Plant sybaritic green clay roses through the center of Cow
Museum. "Peanut" arrives in a fur coat. Some more clay?
No thank you, I have to miss the detestable passenger plane
Of agoraphobic candy, which thousands consider a Mississippi
Hairline. Isn't it customary to Presbyterian Hospital? Larks in a motor.
Water, water, water! Heavenly December. O my sovereign, the railroad
    illness!
Aerate the detached choochoo! The leaves fell, greener than grass-
Colored leather. Can I sell you the wheels, sweet European doctor?

Argentine. Italy. Cairo. Myopia. *The Last Supper.* My twenty-sixth
    birthday.

Nudity Silex Kleenex bells June the Empire State Building.
Do you remember France? Can ants be a peasant? When did the
    daughter of Wendell Willkie walk like green lipstick toward the frogs?
Oh why is the weather no signal of gloom, sweet February twenty-
    seventh? The restaurant would not serve licorice, you remember,
To persons under the age of five, and still I love news! Sweet music of
    cement,
Am I a has-been? What? The water is feeling very pretty and green. The
    gunpowder is coughing beside the submarine archway
Of my twenty-ninth birthday, sea lion, cloudburst November! Did the
    bullfrog say he had something he wants to celebrate? Well, come on!
We can't stand here forever smoking bumblebee cigarettes!

The Man

PENIS

Dancing away from your cars by the frond of the sea I live;
The ramparts are pure rectitude: cut parachutes and deep-sea powdered
    sugar,
A fine run in the silence of the rain—

ARM

          O blue cosmos
Run and financier! Why, there is a France of my up-and-at-them tomb,
A lemon-ray of surreptitious canal sound
Which hops into a series of helpless land.

MIND

I am the mind, dazzling mind reader
Chorus girl in frame-ups landslider
Definition by teacups heavier
Than your Pompeii.

FINGERS

Shorthand the substitute ring me a rose panorama
Climbing western and shirt helpless
The beachless cat. Tomorrow containers!

FOREHEAD

Ocean of Nibelungenlied! Romulus
Satie Mellon canard shoeflex Greene
Dairy farmer. Virus.

NOSE

Oregon bell and carpet.
Leftover silverness. A bell. In a carpet.

EYE

He walks to containers. When the dancing tulip overflows.
The restaurant's a son today. It is sun today.
We throw its overwhelming into the free top that overflows
Blue, violet, purple, everything, the Caribbean ovaries.

OVARIES

What is it? Why am I here?

WRIST

A longer knee events will stop confines orange
Orchestra chocolate logy and snuffly contagious cough.
Reference.

TIBIA

When the foreleg is blue
Covering the lanternslides with fluff country
Panoramic Canada seventieth
Catalogue white swans beer barrel publishing mouse ditch
Wristwatch.

KNEE

With fennel pals the ranch.
The best nights in Arabia. Cotton punches. Rearward actions.
Possibilities will not grumble toward the cheated giraffe
Quietly bursting the cactus with tweezers of cherries,
Just as I cannot remember my norm.
Was bent like this? and is unlike this? Cardboards
Jinglebells and playing cards,
Showing bleachers in light glass.

KNUCKLES

The benches have always been auctioned.

SPINE

The backache penny come niche a lesson
Boa constrictor easel pretzel nylon preaches ruffles
Dance elevators less and more dark
Sassafras relieves me foghorn parenthood quietly duck
Penniless master and a nincompoop hallway
Which seasons come into and look.

HEART

Leopard spots. Why not be a dancer?
Trim summer. Is the hookworm conceived as a relative?
Bust the ocean. In Canada when they say "opera," she brings the nurse.
When silence intimidates the two opium eaters. Rats' legs for breakfast.
Tar and feather the oak tree's builder. Let your mind wander.
Over there. In all kinds of weather. Candy strips them. He builds a glider.
The bell-buoy is a captain. Hate the ocean's builder.
We scream to the sun for kindling wood. Suzanne ignites.
Listen when they say "The peach is hollow"
Because they're lying. Speak of the Renaissance. Describe the feeling
    beneath five layers of snow.
When you are in Romania, be facetious. And they will love you there.
Office furniture. Sailboat's blue mints. Calico shovels. Evening and
    Ireland.
See me handspringing my lookee breast of copper!
The larks bring me,
The dazzling earth has wended
Sunder. I ate lunch in the popularity engine.
She passed the benches. A dog raffle just ended. Your song can't feel the
    motor. The referee has overalls.
Marching beside me I felt that breast of onion!
Looking into the trees. The afternoon was a sundial. Our wheels came,
    too.
Suddenly my answer was changed: the shooting lemons ate whiskey a
    sheep gave a hornet publicity! an architect fell from his office!
Chloroform sat sweetly amused: O ranch houses of green snow

Lectures, castles and rotations. Luminous yet fearless bevel,
What are we? You white bowlegged valleys! I am the happy rose
The working classes have arisen like bright
Seals, and burned the ships whose dark
Indications of blood swing cars by a mere nostalgic smell. Weaken,
   distinctions,
While passionate light
Darkens the formations. There is a pig on the fortifications.
Remember the star of Bethlehem? Cut dead the commander of the root.
Stand on this pier. Summer now brings its roomy cathexis.
By night the elephant is heard, and by day the water. Now it is day, she
   must depart. That way they hear nothing. It is a concert.
From far over the desert a crocodile begins. When they called on one
   another last Easter, it was a rooster. Now a carpet begins to unfold for
   them.
She wants to be the first. He watches her like a cicada; and when he is no
   longer interested
The waters flee with them like sundials. The green cities sit down and
   laugh. To grieve in that climate!
He gives her a pair of angels. They vanish like originals. All is dark . . .
But last summer, I swear,
I heard a voice saying, "Blundering
Coma dancing wild ineptitude, seriousness cars delve orange white
And mother-of-pearl kimonos bleeds delight.
Investing aorta kimono suttee's quietness healthy pianos
Nought handles them for me like shoes."

TEETH

Coldly the knife is Montana

TORSO

Run by the rink lace

HIPS

Orchestra when foetal ice

THIGH

Carnival handball football millionaire
Yes I gave all my gold gives to
The chest, the shoulders, the armpits, the ears, and facial hair

EAR

We hand together

FACIAL HAIR

Love and laughter

ARMPIT

The Earth Mother of silent things

TOE

Bastinado potato

SHOULDER

Boiling

PALM OF THE HAND

Lobster scenario

HEAD HAIR

And can't one gold give will not
Ecstasy domino shoe foot quiescent

REAR

Not to banister forever and ever the bare

SKULL

Rusting of hennaed springtime
Into an act the foot
Wills?

THUMBNAIL

Yet how can we be silent . . . ?

When the Sun Tries to Go On

And, with a shout, collecting coat hangers
Dour rebus, conch, hip,
Ham, the autumn day, oh how genuine!
Literary frog, catch-all boxer, O
Real! The magistrate, say "group," bower, undies
Disk, poop, *Timon of Athens.* When
The bugle shimmies, how glove towns!
It's Merrimac, bends, and pure gymnasium
Impy keels! The earth desks, madmen
Impose a shy (oops) broken tube's child—
Land! why are your bandleaders troops
Of is? Honk, can the mailed rose
Gesticulate? Arm the paper arm!
Bind up the chow in its lintel of sniff.
Rush the pilgrims, destroy tobacco, pool
The dirty beautiful jingling pyjamas, at
Last beside the stove-drum-preventing oyster,
The "Caesar" of tower dins, the cold's "I'm
A dear." O bed, at which I used to sneer at.
Bringing cloth. O song, "Dusted Hoops!" He gave
A dish of. The bear, that sound of pins. O French
Ice cream! balconies of deserted snuff! The hills are
Very underwear, and near "to be"
An angel is shouting, "Wilder baskets!"

For, yes! he helped me collect our bathers
At the white Europe of an unchanged door
Sea, the pun of "chair"
Lowing the flight-seducing moderate
Can. Treat. Hat-waitress city of water
The in-person tunes, drum flossy childhood
Banana-ing the change-murals off winter
Shy. Hay when when shy. Sick murals. Each
In call tone returns his famous cigarette
In labels the Easter cow stubbed man
Is winter the water treats its gusts, we

Love, up! sigh there is a daw truth, the
Manner singing, "Doe, O flight of pets
And hen of the angel!" black sobs to your poets.
Soda, as Wednesday of the east
Vanishing "Rob him
Of the potato's fast guarantee, court
Of Copernican season planes! O bland
Holly!" The breathing semblance of batteries
To five youth-artists . . . "Is it this inspired
That he runs the tree of bather? Watchman?
Glue." It is, fashion, they have up timidity
South, and the lain thorn, too. A lover's decency
In, bank! We: four: "Paint was everyone's top!"

Bomb, thank you for writing to me.
Oat sad, it was a day of cursing blue
Fish, they reunited so the umpire to finish
The exhaustion of the Packard and tarantula
Parallel excursion. O black black black black back,
Under the tea, how a lid's munificent rotation
Is that, he cries, "The daffodil, tire, say-so,"
O manufacture-clams building! Some days are
A fox of coolness and crime. Blot! Blot!
The wind, daisy, O "Call me up, I am
Listing beneath the telephone bat, some
Drum, death and resurrection," what hay ballpark
To forward the punch-mints! O hat theory
Of the definite babies and series of spring
Fearing the cow of day admonished tears
That sigh, "Blue check. The tan of free councils
Cloaks the earth is hen blond, oh want
The dye-bakers' coke and hilly plaza, too
Sunny, bee when halls key tuba plaza corroboration
Mat nickels." O tell us the correction, bay
Ex-table, my cocoa-million dollars! Next
To. O dare, dare-Pullman car! The best way

You howling confetti, is "Easter tray,
As moat-line, promise." How teach the larks!

And, dame! Kong swimming with my bets,
Aladdin, business, out Chanukah of May bust
Sit rumors of ethereal business coo-hill-green
Diamonds, moderns modesty. "There sit
The true the two hens of out-we-do maiden
Monastery belongs to (as! of!) can tin up off cities
Ware fizzle dazzle clothes belong (hand) the hearse
Walls bee bleed, pond ancient youth!" Who're
The den from coffee hanky *hofbrau*, at
Hint-magistrate. O bursar, off
Dollar rainwear, the itch; majesty summer that
Cough lady climate. Magisterial dandy. Apes. Ducks.
"Wanting, Satan, to mark glow-Virginia
A stair, this doe, Virginia. The sea cots
Magisterial lent 'who're' dodos. Aga Khan!
Mutt! the saint of perfect 'more oh' limpidity
Sand, 'bower,' hot, lens, O jetties
And sun rows, calming the Endymion, fair, peaches'
Aspirin" hare, "lewd 'ain't him' summer hat hit
Dulls." They are bottles looser than, pow! hair
Open-necked Kokoschka, leaf, deers, and.
Ashes. Lights. Who bouquet of till stomach
Llama-periwinkle, engine! as under the
Lore "happy mew" inventive "haven't" stalls sprint.

"O goddess handkerchief quartette and the pyramids
How uncommon is your silence amid the pimples
Of today where a skirt pencils your dismay
To the blankets of seemly wind, log-rolling
Foolishly the polka dots of this purged atmosphere
From everywhere, darling time limits! she-planes, and
Pear-planes! O closet of devoted airplanes
How dismissed the reciprocating Congo has to seem

Amid these pans! Ha ha they are the pyramid
Of my strings' dorothy weak hell of youth
Mango, cob, district, lode, shimmy, charmed banks
On a bin of streets." Is Moscow walk,
O lacks? I noticed you on an
Unbearably fast Pullman train, you
Muttered, "India," and bicycles parked in snow
Near the pancake's face, graceless perimeter
Of Count "Blotter," and Prince "Dit-
To," O "O pray"-rhyming cow manufacturer,
Began to wear, science and youth, oh
A pin's aspect, *The Merchant of Venice*. O sods
Of the blameless Atlantic! O murder of the tools
The cosmopolitan lint. Now. Rose bastardy
Millions and millions. She lends me the
Militia of. Bent cow pastures cough grape lights.

A horse is waiting for the submarine's
Feathery balcony. The hollow castle, like a boat
Filled with silliness, is more sand than flag, its
Loose earl phones, "I am dedicating this stanza to you
Marching prince of hacienda quoits. In each bank
An October of pitiful sand is going to be hidden,
Like the midafternoon quietude of the elephant
Who wishes to be indentured, the foolish cosmos
Of the conch for a "soon patter" 's ear life, lad
Of penny, ear, and dock roses, and went to
Ran, sheep, kindness! O black kindness of the hot
Bugle sea-pal ditch-mite hem-location of
Pre-glove. Each birthday momentous peach stanza
Its bother. Llama llama llama llama llama, D,
A, B, O, F, C. Guns
Of pill will! Lint! Where it shows sane
Cat air bench, yas, dash, hoop, *Hamlet*
Of dirty cow-epigram refills, O why are we here?
Bench, dirt, majesty, science, flu, pier,

Sin of "at"s, boo, billboard's ragged canto
Ocean, bitch! "Lousy mineral that makes me shy
Of steering hot flags, mud, who, tin, blue
E calm April hat sky." Hour of. The. Hour
Bong! spins of denying catechisms, Persian pins!

In the St. Patrick's Day parade
I saw a pillow there. It had financial
Dogs! the earthworks did film its plaza! O cross
Head of the pennies' infant rubber sweet
Unglazed pyramidal announcing shaggy deserted melodies
Of "Kismet!" For who now talks of fate? O backs
Of the leaf resisters, blond south of tea
Remembering the bouncy fox Oh night at now he
The office Indian, bingo! What bashful brute
Hints, Oh they are sobbing, kings
Of everything, from aspirin to shoes, and that's
Because, locks of rhubarb with tin
Joys, town of the hateful bust, "Is," ant
Monitor like a sentence's Chinese
Terse cloud. "Weight, honk of deceiving bats, O shelves
Of the earth's tiniest bridges, the memory of short
Faces, are there still linens in your places
Crossword palaces blankets or bent crowds
Of rats, like a billion speeding prescriptions
For gout! O mass of closed bores! Knock
Knock." "The memory of finance is bare, like
A rock substituting for pencils in
A Midsummer Night's Dream. The crow
Flies, but. Harbor. Gold. I am straightening the lilies!

The hill passes for college life. Oh! My
Silver socks in this state of frost. The bed
As of course. The bin of cleavage hat low forest
Adze. A Canada of deceiving forest
Whose hail is the bench of golf links likes

The bad Egypt of a. Howdy, house! Gorilla.
Youth. Fable. Detective. Fur fur fur fur, fur
Midnight. Oh he shot out him like China vast detective
Yelp coop. Dance. Dance a. Bitter California
Of hen-walls, feet, and. Orchard. Ocean.
Oh speed the bench, the district has climates of thyme,
Banquets of fortune, stiff dictators of pep!
Yo-yo, that hen-weaving uniforms, O cloudburst!
"Him, nog, bad, evil, dump, soup, clogs
Stichomythia of brocaded hogs. Show me the yell-planets
Of calked mud and disintegrated satisfy show-people uppers
Of dynamo-isty troglodyte fanny
Mill hock, Jutes, and yell-fanciers
Of many scientific clue-desisters matches prints
On lonely flotsam hoops beside the maggot dusk
Of parachuting dampness, figurative
As lost mints,—howl, sea! The barrow of fulgurating
Plinths are unupbraided by the fat
Kittens of uniform lightning." Sheets mortify!

Is there nothing that gives that "in" a clue,
No moth or beautiful "sock" flower? Wigs, O
Tables of plastered asters, mastery
Of the wig-and-dog show, "But there's no breast here
Of limp or smoky factories, like a cot
Of seasonal folks, the benedicts' brightest, hate!
Lethal. Haps. Ocean bitter song phone cows
Delvage fog's." I see the cancer in your poetry,
Sunflower! O the hair-raising cuckoos in a flake
Of snow, they are bending the rifles in Caucasia now
While while. "The underwear finishes snow
Lately, of outstanding Finland. Earth. Wire. Mottos.
The fish are as warm as painted suggestions
For finishing. Hill. Hip." Oboe! Rebus!
Preposterous rhinoceros of a pilgrim's happiness
At being chef! O tan, bonfire of time's worsted ships!

Your feet in marriage! "We" is being offered as a
"Chicken coop." "Well" is a "bare
Night," "too" is a "cashier's first blossom
Crossing the soft marine Atlantic as the bosom
Of 'cheval' and deepest classicism
Wants the cold and bay-leafed sitting room
Of room" and the "day" is "neck of east
Living beyond," "shower" is "blank peanut, the calm sheep's force."

Blanch tepee rose agora wheelbarrow filled when
Lace temerity ex-"gyp the blond
Stair toe sky's morose tea" clouds, lover
From the sixth Caspian, tombs, and straw, "O store
Of lambs, dream of pads, my! Bucharest of
Decaying lamps' ridged colonic soul ands tear
Pleaser, that locating Solomon, there is *Much Ado
About Nothing*,—sandwich of cars, hag! as we or
Limited true hot people lemons, Shasta is too
Faster the, sip! yo-yo! holly! wheat! man ho high he
Blimp on top of Canada demon, nineteenth, lace, and
Scoptophilia of deserting pins, "I forgot he was dead!
They passed me on the way to my own funeral
Of top hats' tree don Samara cocoa Western heart and
'Paper' phlogiston maps of 'pea'-steep yo-yo banners
Of 'grew' badly, the socks' man-apes, difference
Sea canyon." Hats! hacks! heads! Is buzz. An
Cow-oyster, dollars! alimony of disease-art-lemons, O
Poo, the knack of name's plate's poodle, "Ends" is
Sang, "House! mate of jim-jam corralling puce
Teak!" Out! Badder, yell-place nick and socker-
Glow, each is and, joyous handlike knickers
Cuckoo. "How could you have gone, bitter
Roistering hint glove task phone 'ache' factory hoop device?"

Spot, "kee," sun. My hand of devoted hands
Babel sick, yowl earnest "bee"-boat, seven, connote

"Yoo-hoo" of a gray, bad "bat" disk "bat" boat key
Helen, Sue, loss, sea "hoe" "doe look"
Of candour. Yards! unbalanced "Percy" yachts dew
"Harold," Otto, change "curve" troop boat "tree"
Ben, the middle of. Oh stop, dancing, "Sidney," black
Tripes! Hollow pigeons. "Loma," itching porch and meadows'
"Chinese characters from block, land odd dress, wolves'
Hill." "Bob" at sharpens "this" canoe, Betty
I'll "Molly" hick tables' dumb morrow, "fit" Cajun-
Money, South hat A.D. Maria Theresa, honds
Of blue "gal," hurting the sable boats ump George
Of receding pets "Fairy Story" act is "then" "Chloe"
S bottle E honor house banknote with stiff looks!
O blinding treason, tee-clouds "It is better to give
Banjo receive" pop, gardens! "Herb," doe, us, in, ace
"Cass Horse." Peace! pans! jonquils
Of a body's discrete jungles, nert of the duped torture journal,
"Orange Nights," where a coma's weak cigars
Sped the ice drink saving hoop, "Calm city climates
Of porch-limiting beach" a bonanza of falsefaces, to "we
On the earth, holiday of canoeing rockets
Bang." College the yo-yos. Leaf! Ape! Eldorado millions!

The worried Chelsea "runs not our dance, fee
Lymbariums," Norway my Chelsea, blunder-
Kensingtons. Ah, certain lamb of Sheba
And darkly papers, his, career-dancing cocoa
Matchsticks' genteel
Disintegrating plaza of bound, round,
Choosable tins, diamond
As the choice of carfare, hungry
Jewish flanks, tanks of chaste liquids
Sent by the Pope, O dirty youth movements
Of the wild cursing salad
Of sidewalks' bending
Few romantic ears, Sheba O hens' bonanza

Of Cuban cash registers! What bad religions,
Bowls of hat, and touring columbarium religions
Syntaxes the parachuting mysteries.
Of. Bag. Tellurium. She. Bounced. Across.
The stairs! O kremlin of distinguished blotters!
I was touching your cosine, thou best of the kittens'
Tub airy Andes oar-pardoned rooms. Despotism
Piano kimono. Calm men, an "airy frightened cars
Of peaceful me 'how is fair?' Perspiration at big clouds.
Hold the play me, again beyond the clam,
Winter. Shame. Cow. Sen." "My railroad turns blue

At the faulty whistles of your ocean, eep! mighty steamship
Of *Child Life* magazine. By the sun of bar May India clues
I fled an midnight's how droopy Silesian clock bear
Carved, sum! tea new possum Colors Change. The big beer
I drank, imagination, when, I felt. The sunrise. Other. My belt."
She puts his clothes into the conversation
As if a pearl fan-danced. She shouts, "Ice water!"
She heeds the fan-dancing of his conversation
As if police force. She shrugs off the angel
Of his interest, blossoms, grow! as though
Seamanship. There are black lintels of clouding clocks
Of banjo dust she marches against the wall.
She sacks the train of swaying logs of snow
In mint apartments, trying to be kind
As mastering easy music. There is a pound of shelves
Which she does not know where to put, therefore
Classical Greeks. As she has painted, every parcel,
So that it resembles a soldier. Shame! Wheel! Shoulder
Of needy clouds! She wanders through
Name, soda, grass day earthing
Nigh if landscape's "cold," "inch," "tough." She inner sun as
Quotes' daring bedroom, air sea
Land beau hop's "consistently" free. O "Crew of dynastic sweeps,
Mayn't we return to the filthy London of your childhood?"

In the submarine hats conversation, beds and.
Oboe den of heathen bonnet floats. Cry,
"Tube, he, S," coptic arrangement of
Pay, he give "Bernard" hill M.I. enemy
Flower. "Jane" pony, O "Russell"! That few hog wild
Saracen bakes gypsy frog "leader of counsel, who
Is brick." White hill hat fools the meadow hat
Fistula bog Greece, ad intention of begonia's
Nameless shoes. "Marsh." Eye crime your bistro,
Mad we am everything. The hot grip
Of clay rhubarb, in cozy suns, of driving birds
At pill alliances, and crazy suburbs. "Hoops
Fight me. Hot. Air. West. O lair, O tamest yak
In air beseeching clarifications' post office
Weak. Dray colossal, hip, emps one clip hasp
C-bars. O Romania!" Yes est.'s talkative brassieres
In wow-cameo flies. Dare. Toe climes
Two D, Florida lake bill-piano. Please, Bill. O
Walls of British enthusiasm. Hill-grown soup,
Time, axe, we are in. How Roman "Shirley
Who was going to place the freight-baked state
Of eight 'do-go-away's onto." Itchy sabbath
Ha, ha. I am fenced in by reluctance
Cuckoo commas, and daring "deceased fences."

Lucky the moaning caretaker, favorite the sea
And numb to dirt, exhaustion, face, each, flax,
Cologne, pitiful comic strips commingling gold
Fracas Endymion dimples with clocklike rhubarb
The cuckoo clock shouts, mad cuckoo clock
Bartender silence-creation "fills." There are.
Homily of shops "mock," dear house of yo-yos!
Horse "nay," a differing comet of yo-yos'
Balanced deserving cheese "giants" cuckoo clock
O matadors! defying and "oh," levels of sweetness's
Cheese. Blah. They are Harry, Susan, Lynn

Blotter. "Major" Blotter, with film of "Gordon"
Cuckoo clocks, the passageway to Easter. Motto:
"Cosine the defeated hips." O pazzling dizzling author
Of *Chow Face, a Nincompoop for Dogs*! "Murray,
Lyle, and Jean" Cuckoo clocks. O Madagascar
Mazda wintry tights. Sascha films
"Ellen's Back," "Eileen's Bock," "the"s, "so"s.
O sartorial "tree"-camps of demanding yo-yos'
Faces of "von Mirror" 's. Hobby. Natal. House.
"Wotan, leaf are my cuckoo clock. Show me, that imp
Cheese! He are forgotten satch bell of a glue bell,
Listener-bell." Train sigh in the "Andy" bell show-off,
Too "Yorick" "Bill." Ding dong ding dong there is the bell!

Stove! you cursing troopers of Egypt
Black, "heart"-egret, result "scowl-balcony"
Midnight, "What" bottles of, looms!
Intelligent valentines, "spent" 's, and "cap" 's!
Hoed youth, not beside. Mineral's little
"Agnes the lea, O terrible Hoo 'Kays' of frost's
My general'll coming down. So match, is
'Pet'-gown, whacking, miss, and four 'got
Ladles.' Danish." What short script "Ha Bessarabia
Ha Bessarabia." Taster of Northern Lights,
The cheerful disuse of Safety matches, the period
Of "Oh I hate the murdered streetcars'
Stove! the blanched pyramid, sounds nice, bee,
Kom Tom, hoodoo, banana class, array, likes who,
Plaza. Carolina of useful fetes O lovely soup the
Carved, gentleman, lonely, of raided springtime
Dance, cocoa-pain! Billonaire loading-guns, is
Bending myopia for glass steaks. Monster veal chops
And mint cuckoo consommé, glass bananas, glass
Oysters and peaceless bicycles, running
To, fats! the train, a glass arch remover, Ben
Loth, light rays, O shoes! 'Rather than kill

Be killed'-store of wavy nickels. Shore! See their
Little hands," the month of coat-Lambeth spare sea monsters!

"A copy of 'Chews' has ripped my cheers a pack"
"The somnolence of Genji" "Hopeful" "Engine-ski-mo
Modern" "German pea hospital" "O cloud binge"
"Country notice mother, 'll take the city
In marriage" "Baked snow" "Empirin tablets
There is a closet of every beneath" "Youthful
Marzipan" "Chow Frigidaire" Now, be uncommon
There is a package of
Red, white, and blue RATS! charging. Houseboat!
Film star! "The eating I mentioned to you
Last Thursday was totally unlimited by
Mediterranean comic billboards wordings'
Sailboats of misdirection, as if soap
'Mocks' the tea-tablets' December wrongdoing's
Bear." He was more British than an icebox. Out
The rats ripped him. Shovel. A pier
Of sudden "Flo" gladness. The minted peach-fly
Sounds, "O badger of repeated adzes,
Longtime, few, hat, het, boat, sand,
Lockers, knee, mistress of Aix, umpire with three shouts,
O blue tapeworm, sonnet of powerful indifference, nest
Of hallways of birthday sheep, soror, tie
On pretty benches lay my ore coaty head
Wind the banjo 'mock-hooped,' Andy dust 'Freemason.' "

Earthworks of genuine Pierre! Molly. Champak's. Egypt.
Esteban Vicente. Melodies'. Cow. Advance is chewing gum.
Saith Bill de Kooning, "I turned my yo-yo into a gun,
Bang Bank! Half of the war close pinstripes.
Timothy Tomato, Romulus Gun." "The magic of his
Couscous masterpiece," saith Pierre, "is apple blossoms'
Merchant marine gun." Ouch. The world is Ashbery
Tonight. "I am flooding you with catacombs,"

Saith Larry Rivers (more of him later on).
There is also some fools laying on their stomachs.
O show! merchant marine of Venice!
At lilac wears a beetle on its chest!
These modern masters chew up moths. How many drawers
Are in your chest? Moon Mullins' Moon Mullins
Put his feet in my Cincinnati apple blossoms. Many
Dry cigarettes have fallen into work's colors. The shop
Of geniuses has closed. Jane Freilicher
Might walk through this air like a French lilac,
Her maiden name is Niederhoffer, she tends the stove.
"O shouting shop, my basement's apple blossoms!"
There is a tiny drawer more hot than elbows,
Season. Number, favor, say. Old winter oh
Winter. The park is full of water veins and
Surly council members, or sad Creons. Sway, unsound airplanes!

O dog! knee-Decembers of an egg-
Sabbath, the dispensaries in a south of foods'
Mailed "bowwow" summer, peripheries. I I
That murders Carolina soup is
Stonding in the ho! of taken columns' dear
Shaken bell of fast! Mallarmé cologne's
Constantinople dove-winter. They say she travels
Like brick ontological ("bay" bay) parlor
Communist hill saber news ape, Otto, Tyrinth
And. What? sweethearts! ember district worm
Hair raising! In the submarine lost blankets
Of Commedia del Arte parachute loop Canada.
The dancers "took" in the forest of Egypt, yes the
Contenting Telemachus of dissenting "bough"
Sweethearts, sweet periods after summer's woe
Season red participles, O manager of Latin
Sights! the worst fevers. "O Soma, delerious hexagon!
How I have been shunted into the batter's box, rats,
On local music, shy motto, tear! sun-wafted tear!

'Brote,' brought, to Columbus!" Oh where is my origin's
Style-raising-disinterest-tack-St. Louis of
Charlemagne true day council of murdered persimmons'
"Eep"? Mother, we are dancing on the closet in
The sway defeat column comma mixed-up oxygen! "Beau!"

O the worst, owl! Car blankets the
Defeats' component lady other slim rose
Racing the bell four warmth May
Tie O banner constancies'
Sharp dens. Away! for you,
Bell! the southern mountains. "Am list" handkerchief
Yo-yo and butlers! "That science of plows
My Endymion, mind, shoes. The air
Rates gold, engine of sigh, cogs, rheumatic
Freight. My hat! His. Seven. Since. Birth of slot machines
Upon a gypsy cola." Vember. No Sept. Oct.
I am bathing the turf in airplanes,
Saith Cary Shivers. What no-man's-land of gout
Hens! "There is a sharp usk to the 'rows-
Me-out-to-his-face,' " O most twins! twins! twins!
"I folded with him shyly Madagascar,
Pots of myriads, pliable rents'
Birth airplanes, and he, he—" Sad crop of
Gentle newspapers, hog! Pleasing air of Chicago
Why, don't run toward me with the
Your handkerchief as Saturday reservations.
Oh now the train is plugging us our shirts'
Pianos', hem fractured dogs. Gold mustard!
"A day is 'what a season' is the temporal doughnut."

"But he lends wing to our murder case" ugh what
China of dancing joke books. Hairline here's the
And melody of hopey rats. Lilacs for your birthday
Sim. O are there sharecroppers of worded sweets'
Nonsense prizing Bibles of glowing beds'

Mild joy dance-incineration, rebus? O Rebus!
Coat of lobsters, flowers, menstruation, leave us
Empty out this dedicating Chaucerian passage they
Often, shower, often, weeds, "manage to cuss," said
"Sid," House of the Gifted Orphan. O bands
Of church, painters of false weeds, mommas of
Country appearance, hay's unclassified wall
Suit stock! Manners! God, General Pershing,
Itch, water, unclassified silver. But you. In.
The sands of, what—shifted bayou bombing like nets
"Samuel." Eat tea sets, love; bother. "Frank" Cuckooclock,
Welcome to the speech of hods. Oh, ow!
The silent merchant is invaded by desperate "send-
Us-up-to-the-woodchuck-for-coat-she-enterprise-
Pin-clue-bock-hurt-Sven white elephant
Of pacing German Childs restaurants, at mint
Concerts to pick at sunrise 'a world's nose,' "
A daisy elephant, the merchant marine of sheds
And dancing nose, commonly "nose of sherbet and 'seems' weather.' "

The yo-yos of Paris knock together in this
In this. "We ran, shuffling, tobacco, sun, hat.
Borderline, pooly collar! Black
Lint! O China! where, poodle, savior, Negro, said,
'Happiest rose and dear buy rosin' " is,
Then they all came together again, in
Out-of-date, "kin," barefoot rose of aints
Shirtwaisted for several union. Where a pin
Montparnasse crutch, "the D.C. roses are
Fat!" Bush! Then I knew. The sixteenth
Bashful locker, the weary "Joanna"
Room Indian was my—palace of leading snow,
How there you are! with matrons
On Tokio seats' south-placated loop columbariums
Is farther gypsy. Oh notice! there are piers
Under, the, shy sweet Elaine, and along, last

Year, about this . . . "Orchard five yards long!
O packed saviors of prickly heat! what from
'Keats' you O nut shoe bandboxing surface
Leopardskin fireproof rose magistrate, deaf
Queneau. O period of conceited shoplifting by
Sham tissue 'pay fear' that with stoves tulips,
'Meddy tears,' 'jan-quills,' and shooting Flauberts
Of 'we-fill' light, O Commonness Very of sheds!"

The yo-yo's mother is not from Paris. She dranks
"Peegs." Left you. I left you. In Russia
Blanket miller floaty. Bay day Canada mirror
Canada be to pare the floatsy rose "buy 'em"
Sudsy landslide marigold woowoo "looks like." This
At the bottom of twins. O. My paper glass
Is Sheridan Square. No, office. Daring Hoboken
Of twisted Studebakers. She fills
A Mediterranean heart with friendly costumes. Baa,
Mirrors the sheep. Nert. There is a carfare in my window
Why in after *is* blossoms. Oh. Brother of turning gold.
The cops began a workout. Cheerless silver
Matches. "A day of foreign roses the sheep
Love clowns the clouds and Major 'T. Cigars'
Works and drinks." A maritime virgin sinks
Beyond the *Leslie C.* O bogs of Syrian dogs
Of marriageable playing togs, Count
Pat, there are Gemini in the faithful seminar
Of serenading teabags' windows' dynasty of hops,
Yes, bather, sermon, untire and so
I think I *can't* understand your bath, know
The Sabine film substitute outside chimpanzee meadows
Of health. That ship is hall of landslide's
Say, Dee, end Saranac ore, "what was," "tint," seas!

Mew. R. We're blood patents that weird pink
Tea—fro, runs "Silo, Bill; tea" Madam steer, shower

Of wear-me-out-in-the-feet-aspirin, satin
Trireme shoe statue might Himalayas its
Tramway scene box. Hill-dog, pay! Grab
The fennel bee of the hollow Macon Subway
New, cockroach of faded ilk, deceased rosemary
London, pens 'draped "golly," and, over
Pied sheep, damn upstairs I see sigh "No umpire
Shovels, Lambeth." Orange magic, sensibility
February amid the strawberries! Raspberries
Mutation moth of a deceptive hillbilly's
Luminous, snow, Cossack, waited, tree. Sense had
Shakes, ovary along, beach, true
Fringe of I May den chorine clockwise raspberries'
Hindrance loop of water Pindar-dependences'
Snowy Sam-a-top of wondrous Thrace
Of if of of of shy's blessings "whin" a cold
Houses of deserted aspirin, cell-less rosemary!
Cinder, hollow, China roseberry.
Rune shelves, a merest baby council-chamber
Motto: Sistine Chapel, "fair weather, fewer deserted
Anywhere comma rosaries, lime-tree ovaries
In quiet subway, hooray, 'Sue' of deceiving umpires."

Wear out Sue, and who is she, wear "Am I?"
To the shirt's dance, south of bells! And the
Myriad of con sister fan hensy. O dotes
Wear climate changes. Wear the Sistine granges!
O matador, the charming "a fear" of bells,
The masonite of deporting bills, goose affair,
Hen affair, shirtly, hoop, a client, balcony
In central "horse." Oh the sea of pipe
Criticism is a nest egg of hags'
Merchant marine shelf confusion. "District Ninety,
Howp, this is Commissioner Jimmy. Leap the darts."
Chancellor of my ballad's celluloid hearts,
Lump together! "And the bear wangled from the goose

A distant holiday, mirrors which are also shoved
High, daring hearts, and the plasma of cupidity, dire
Tin, shocking hooves." Mercenary strangers! she
Is Caspian and underwear, the sentences
Of "How pipe! how district October page nice
German loop! Gaga midgets' tornado as
Niece of. All your. January musicians of
Tan!" At summer he figures, "Tornado
Tomato, badgers of defeated licorice, some
White bloomers of breathing calamine, determined
Shoulderies of demented cobwebs, sea-high feet."

As Copenhagen, O remains of the "ear
Factory" tunes "Quiet Venice, door to seem the door
Able plaza toe, Sim, quiet orange Egypt,
O birth of the oranges, range of fells
'Coalmine'-quacking dirndls of 'thy shifting smack
Smearer than the "kill" of soup,' liberty to sigh
'Positive bracelets, of oranges, the rattlesnakes,
Forget my key, O den of deceased lemons, den
Opera quietly no-place Pullman car if lemons
Really.' " But he prints has hit is nowhere is
As defending Egypt rugs from under the moor or
"Solid beans of Stonehenge," the cow's
Mulatto imperialism, dancing "life invaded shirts,"
O merry chowdog of receding pills,
Why aren't you back at home? Emergency. His share
As bursted hens the decency "of" lemons, now
The "Blenheim" of conceited automobiles'
"Feet air" doors, a Sanscrit "lying at" his feet
Mirth filling the cat racial "doughnut" memory
Yes yes. How am I stupid dear strawberry
Mountain? Has the day "knucks" rarely
Money reason and show "sea" "hoop" cheery fountain
Of Moscow Saturdays, orchard "wain" my love
Is lemons, Norway, hamp, sure? Location bigs

The "three" soap stairs, and "my" tower sunbeams
Escaped of devoted Swedeland O sharing miss—
House "bather baby" pot, millionaire pages
Under a shouting lemons of disapproval
An military! shoes baby to take off
Lilac is courtroom cool Decimber house on
"Quaffed" judge-simplicity, Apollodorus'
Cuckoo top hat birthday landslides of
Of! Wills! O tubes of disastrous London by
North us, codpieces of benching cloud-
Blameless surf disk-formation as
Shooting the comet "Birthday" cement feet's
Doorway, "Santa," build of repeating tassel-
Commenced shirt yo-yos, unMarseilles! These say
Or after air is. "Rambling" "my pin" "the forest"
"How nigh he ware D (cooling) con Santa
Dim yay! yay!" Hopeless, bobbed air
Eighteenth "Sir Face Din" cows limb
Couscous ick's howed maritime BABY
Sham "tree"-blamable, as midnight summertime
"Safely to film a cow with hair-beautiful-
Dense potters of shoe-breeze balcony out is
Baby to defy delicate; merchant, O talcum oranges
Of the sea-as, wholesale face at sighs wheat dove!"

"The church of spended babies is all right,"
The peanut telephones, merry peanut, "If."
Our, climate, promotion, Sundays, "If"
When the bursar's damp clubs. Shyest cups
In the spirit of sound effects, dandelion "If"
And "Stevie" asks somewhere sweet streetcar
Of street-sweet car as the valence of talcum
Moderation of cosine's talcum. "These
Lemons if, stereotyped. Buy now, in shame,
Thick quietness's first linguistic dove." Every-
Thing possessed. O donation Frank O'Hara to

Lightness. Donation, "Sea
Of quietness's dirty froth parachute with yellow
Disinterest buckaroo-plazas O shy pal
Of mirthy telephones, and gyroscopes! our bittersweet
Goodbye! The bun-sleeve hopes you with its heart!
Of plotted asters, O my faded shark! Den, feasible,
Quieter than the pinpricks in the onion
Saying 'Chicago! Chicago!,' ass from a million years
Ago!" How that dove is corduroys, and how
The ship walked through its sweetheart, "Custard
Of the Blenheim caves," he counts on screaming, first
Reason to year, up! the egg, changer the
Cosine of since, dank pool, cot, now the waves' growing tenderness!

There is a plinth I am hopping. You undress
The years, O waggons. There wind bottles
Off deceiving minnows. Frankness, deer, what sleds!
O Shalott of shaggy air, "Lumber-time," and
"Jeering, Jeering Notation." Now we are
Ours in the air! The murderess eats clams
In Norwegia, cement of our burning frankincense!
Cantata of American troubadours,
What north woods? "Outward the cuties of concrete
Pure she's-castanets, bowing toward the summery Irish
Stairway to gypsy phonetics." They murder my clouds
In your "fancy delectable conceit gyroscope
To 'tossed where we bled, ache, burning dinosaurs!' and
'Sheds of that blinding pace.' " My my-nurse,
Austria. "It was a season of candy dinosaurs;
I picked up my bottle and fell
Danger candy dinosaurs. You teach me German
Phonetics." They labeled beneath the church-road table.
That was Greece. It was the first Shasta.
He built an envelope. She watched him beneath her eyes.
"Those are lids that were his kind effects
O summery gypsy phonetics!" Now she drinks coffee.

The Irish have been murdered. For copying.
O the sailboats of her eyes, a Southern Cross!

"In growing Canadian fields of stupid iced tea
I wavered. Could I be the
Magic scoptophilia pilgrim of growing pirates'
Nest? Lackawanna Mary-go-home three million.
O January month of cloudy lightning
Future, lint of mountain hat-bag
And Ceylonic wheels, murder my postage stamp
For me!" There is a Bessarabia of guns
Pinpointing his deluded shoulder. Ouch! Tristan! Men
Calmly disturb the delicious pirate. Women
Find his grape shirts, orange
The distance is, filing, motto, pea, chariot's
Coercive May in line cuckoo clocks, that
Summer is here! "Embasket the gloated fibs,
Realize the cashier's desk, flub the sea
Of rotating pipes, hat-joyous arranger of thugs'
Repine, oh shop in the germ-surveying
Lulu-bards, plinth my hat-surveying figs'
Youth pot-parks, darling the arranges of sog-
Mittjoy is Germany weather, dank gods of
'People will knock glow home, match, symphony
And Constantinople of conceiving pods' dancing
For joy in the middle, loves' car-in-case
Sea, dirty roses of plowing space, mailman-songbook,

Earthenware, clockwork, hen-disinterested
Pittsburgh, shy mirror of hats, O
May! in the delicate burnoose of chocolate
Crayons, council chamber of tea, owls, blood,
Champagne, dear 'Old Sturbridge,'
The glass nude confined in a sailing blanket of
Hats' sun, with what curves I.
Heater, blondes of questionable space! Cow-

Fair of cheated, and nursemaid of sweet blondes!
Month of blondes! Bombs which mislead, chatter,
They *dire la malade n'est plus à deranger, ça, ça*
Alors, éteinte comme elle est, oh la la, morte, comme
La malade n'est plus bombs away sea of lurch
And cloud hill-her blondes the quiet sarsaparilla
Near a thug's twins. *The Merchant of Venice*, O
Landslide of decayed strings, shafter
Menner and gone. They talked at the
Dove, 'we' Danube, yare, mischievous yo-yos'
Plaque of recent parents the dirty cloud, mustard thrill,
'As' beach of china, a bird's cleanliness
With birds', chewing gum and (banjo of peels)
O Florida's pockmarked coast. Magic
Apes! other quiet climate inside my collar
Blondes me, hoop! knotting car fierce damped cuckoo clocks,

The stevedores banyan 'trees,' boughs, terebinth
Is longing for 'cleanliness, near or down the nights'
Rag of your night is we batters' terebinth
Of sorrowing sighs, 'Leaf, matching and cow,' the dense
Blotter, which tears, O bag! the rooms polka
Of feeding clowns', bitterness, 'ant'-terminations'
Sunrise. What is the use of disease
And this floor? O barristers in the
Europe of a blond dress, American chiefs'
Shower of bears, tears, bland
Modesty of the 'cokie's' cities' sherbet
Feathers of deknife, chowmiller and bath
Tundras, of devoted. Stare, China, at these uniform clouds.
The murdered potatoes are keeping the sun
From its sun, common marriage of simplicity with
Sulfurous. 'Ant's'-disease, is the sun. Sang 'Blondes
Of the breathing can.' Seldom 'you' buy
The sharecropper, O sea! 'Daniel of our
Lions' den,' church of dismayed lint, how tall

The periods are, Romulus and Remus of the
Joking casket! Tennis on fields of lint, 'The
Sun.' O lost back, the matadors of toothless cities!
That is 'worm-pretty.' Headless. Mayan
'Soon' of shore, the quietness of Silence Mare Show

Lamps is, monitor of a chapter-freed delphinium,
Delphos of the merry climate of 'What are rules?'
Reason, linen mead, air, ribs, oh the size of silence
Bearing shods! Let me, settee of defeated 'rows
Away, photo,' quit the Hernani and
'Tea'-deadening shower, Mazda, climate, quits,
Denver, rose 'like the black youth
Of copper, this summer's solid quince, and colleges
Of delighted silence, pin, carry me and use the
Pan complimenting your head-
Line of frozen knee-bullets' shirts'
Quietly delphinium and freedmen faces.' So,
Sorrow magic greens." The winter ends, as
A pig discovered America last night. O boys. Now.
Samuel. Ocean. Clever wisteria of logs. Hoe
Of tweet-tweet hens hat charming college-bunny
Nexus-filler, hooray-pillow, llama and
Dewy-faced limerick of charts. For pyjama.
Semantics of village, *joyaux*, buildings, "loops."
Rather. "Heaven" clutches his head. Sweet summerwear.
"Comma, I showed you different climate, whoopee
Step-the-soap stairs. Wow languorously lethal.
Tyrinth. Difficulty sweater. Parachute, nun, "Queen
Bath," oh, arrivals in the potatoes of. The city.

Sails! earth, "how perished laundry?" Bin. Clad.
Coconuts, binge, paratroopers, wheat,
Castles of dancing tattoos, even paratroopers
Of an orange's daily injustice. Malabar. Shredded Wheat.
Lemons what "few," kiln am "burr day
Umber" members deSouth, helmet, on "teached

Imagination, calm." O dirty shrapnel of conceding
Skates' first laugh "after" youth fields'
Lint queue of "sat"-bath, "after," shrapnel
New, cracks "after," bug retires. Sheeps' lackey! yo-yo!
Dock. Rays. Easel. Set Andes
Shirt-manufacturer decency of cold,
"Hens. May-nifty, motto. Donatello, sway now
Terminals," cups of French steam! April blotters
Miss you, Donatello yo-yo. O black literature! Back
India yo-yo home. Matches, wee. Colonel. Asleep.
In. Wee. Comical landslides of
Pretty legislature. Bent "lions' " Algiers, Illinois.
Conch of sashayed pill. White is appearance
Germany bathroom cow nutty ashamed personal
It's purple. Breaking into my heart like a
"Climb this blotter of permanent yellow lace,
Weary old *comédie*." Am burr lace. Desk. Pick
Up the yo-yo. After. Hebe. "Thanks," in this purple hour!

Bong! went the faery blotters; Ding Dong! the
Country of Easter! shore! each toes
The marriage bin, shouts of "Conch!" "Ruthie" "Lurks
Behind the 'pea' is basement's Illinois
Obtuse radio lithogram!" "Coptic!" and "Weak Beddoes
Less-us-the-shirt!" Ran behind me-Vishnu, all
Summer. Closet of how it seems! O bare necks
In October, closest apparent "film star" of the
Buffalo. Peter of Carolina's neatest snow-
Pier condescension. O haughty chapter how
Clear was as apparent cruelty, bonnet,
List, tackles the lace. Hump chariots the summer
Either desires. Ether, so tall
As ice, sees her cuckoo hooves at desire
Margin. Amour dodo cranberries. There
"Art," "blamelessly," cashes, D's, wed's hat's
HEADS! Joyous midnights, different clams!
Oh the word "flotation" 's cosined beaver rotation beneath

The "seelvery" dog-freight cars, mammoth
Stomach-quiz-raspberries we parent
Cuckoo Mary coast-disinterest verst of "cheese" diversed
Flags of the "comma stare" rewhipped
Georgia of teaching cash registers to "hat" side
Of pale "plates," the bitter "nurse" southing "ha"-green "stangs"
     forward!

O badgers, badges, bats, bags, bags is,
Black, blacks, rats is, as, is as, as, is,
Badgers as, is, is, bridges', bags, bags as is
Business of the fourteen (I noticed "Henry") badgers.
Dark plantation of these furious sidewalks! First
Lifted-up usual "Mamie"-hello, dockworker,
Pancake, silliness, feet-locker, lower-class,
Power-gasp, Kokomo, dithyramb kimono. Whang
Bang! collar, bleachers, parachute, delicacy,
Noun, Janice, dental work, siren, sirens, boulevard,
Tarragon, limp May, wine, decency, earth, mountain
Sidewalks, decency, earth, sidewalks' happy sirens,
"Match wrappers! Match wrappers!" Juno, Janice,
Meat hooks, Elaine, lilacs, parapsychological
Cocoa-distinction plasm, jowls of the seedy grocer,
Monday, disinterest, sea ramparts, banjos, groups
Of pineapply-flavored Jericho lemons. Sleep, sleep.
Merchant marine O thousandth freight in Venice,
Cutie, waters, envelope, chapter, thousandth,
Frigate, sleep-resisting billboards, if mountain
Choreograph, seventeen, resisted. Maldoror,
Shirt ads, of wintry face. Council of blackest
Dogs, sleep, is slain. Cutie. Is resisted.
Visit is. Disinterest. False solomon's seal. Go to sleep.

"I arise from dreams of thee, open-air bell
Ohm tiny match his hat duke wheat son
Wild, Peru. Genji of deciding cups'
Care-cup! noun, as ash, flossy hit"; we

Are the hips of everybody's son; nat-
Urally, leaves a sun, day, choked up, read or, is
Anybody! disturbs naturally "th' sweater
Empties the feet in Yarrow. Hal is musically
Very is, jay weird sight of tomorrow
Bannisters." Surge of banditti, oh,
Sweethearts. There is a seventeenth moon deciding
Wheat-ministry-triangle-deranged churchmouse.
End tea socialist clubhouse before you begin
Eating sweaters. The pears are dancing. What rain?
Manna isthmus, dose of climate, way
Orchard noun and in the Swanee sheep. "Baked
Hats! to arrive from seams of tree
Service, town. Anne in delighted orchids. O mashed
Lakes, biers, seventieth pyre of green
New Yorks, loam 'where beautiful
As Eden, voodoo shades in Charleston religion? "Sue"
Weak, daring, America,' " and the raided shocks
Hobo, mean, soporific knicks. Marjoram chinchilla. O sea
By quirk, calmness, shy, "Indeed-ape," bob the thousand!

Orchard of the deceiving ant, penthouse in
Mere cunctation of "we" browing air-patience
Toreador matches-siblings "Oliver" Bowlingballs
And "Mary" Isn't-working-the-dream-downward, come home, shake
Fiery sea aspirin, as "I'm using a the Lake Poets'
Win-bandit-flowers!" From Huey's casement
March, April, and solemnity, the cool sincerity babies
Up upon chair-car, flying through nameless England! Banjo
Of peace! monthhood! ooh, Soho! yak of the German clams!
Pack of "The Diamond Ships" ' bursars-maying-cards knee
High true she "Boston" domino! "Shirt can I wear, is
The cue ball's dirtiest Delibes." O monthly
Syntax of a florist's cones, "Charles" with the blink
Face, characters from Canada! Dizzy the Charleston
As pink merchants, green you are faded yoo-hoo!
The classroom, O pitch! these surface classicism

Plotting the tube's creation from conscious mattresses'
Series of dismaying springs. O logs, manner, and T-
Square. "The horrible ditch is ended. Now
Yo-yos air parachuting flamingos, job hunters
Have breached their blue home; nominally the cuckoo
Is such a chair-far hunter. Wintry the tables blue
Deer, in the tables of Z-dancing 'Koko' are here,
Sew, too, shun the further 'ants-eat-people.' " "Loud and bill!"

Bandana of cavey sea-tins! pyjamas! ladder on
"Eek's" bugle call of shallow GLUE, PIER, SOLDIER, and
SPILLWORT dirtiest case of the marshmallow
Sin language, merchant marine of chows! Back, lurid
Leaf of the Chair FINANCE! O
Santa Claus can heaps behoove love cemetery
Gypsy. Market of playing Beans' Research, Baa
Lethal tagsheep. Erp. "Kill my shabby
Dog with careless BEANS. Or jellybeans
Will complicate four research-
Pilgrims in, lazier than the, GREEN
Rebus of opium. Oh, daze!" Why shirts came RED
As youth ex-Canadas, shallow doggest dream—
Lamp, "Sunday I boxed a COLITIS pinprick,
Shore!" Ugh-row of the lazy-towels-when,
GERMANY and CALIFORNIA again! The RIGHT
Beans hill know a banjo toga-conference
Disinterest. Sherman for president! Surface
Chow, O green! air, go away. BATTERS
Up! "She decides to become the climate
Of ARABIA, she banisters two CALIFORNIA and
Diamonds. Sense-tea-wear bay dun off oof focus
And becomes WELL-BEING, the turtle
Of grace, knickers, and cactus. SHE has no colitis!"

O Barrymore, the choosing of a place
Beside the Russia of dirt's Coliseum. ADS

For nothing! chowdog chowdog as "this" hearing aid!
Manhattan, you are the author!
Blankets, chancellors, film-dogs, nurse-waves, banjo-
Stevedores so cashmere as red, O billboards the
Passage of "gorge" delicious-makeup season
Shasta of pirates' disinterest "tornados" and
"Shack of hued blimps!" O best
Bench, Bessarabia. They are watching the feet on
My eyes; the dust is resenting halva, "Marriage
Of Figure." Oyster had gherkins and his eyes
Were breathing like the Chesapeake and Ohio
Railroad. Dog pats him to slip, certain lilies
Of Canada blind HIM. God, what an awful night
To be the terrible illness of Southey's dog!
They are picking out some lanterns is Nephritite
Dirndl is connoted handkerchiefs. Why, Violet!
You here among the summers' dogs? "White?" "Why an
Heartache isk more total than bananas'
Windy" violets freeze! Say, there is a
Sharecropper of total blackness. Uncle Steven's
Hat! We never expected kin to blouse
Arabic, up! O "Ladislaus, the loss is gone to sleep!"

He: "The strawberries are putting." She: "Brilliant Egypt,
I wonder about the ladies' dancing carfare
That Percival said was 'baby us, brilliant oranges!'
They say for my sake she wore a silver kerchief!"
Bill! How Mordred to Arthur you my handy gear
Of fair sexiness, she thinks. He places: "Lock
In the baby of you fair oranges. Lock
In the baby. O doubts, mirlitons and foghorns!
They say he had appeared to be a bench,
But Canada toured him in her brilliant pockets
And he became her 'Solitude,' a large, furbished painting
That used no hands the way anciently oranges
Listed to the bugle call's left." Allah, frogslegs!

They are so tear-bitten! Water as lovable clues
Deceives-as lines there cuffs showering "purple
Scientists who tea their frost"; lobster,
Why haven't you been invited to the painting?
"I was too cross, and too yellow. They really
Aren't the two you sawed in half yesterday. Watch
My pins!" Lands! I saw a lobster leap the gas range,
A merchant of March. "She sold me two red kimonos,"
A dear thinks, "and yet, when I walked the Allahplaza
Remembering dirt kangaroos, I forget my name.
Is it 'Shorty,' or 'Polly,' or 'Julie'? Oh it may I am the nurse!"

O soul of all my life, ah solo flight
Beyond the Mexican blue! "It is predicted
Giraffe-gorilla-that-I-am-to-be-killed. Lethe
Corral me 'now' the burnoose other blue
Landslide!" Mud, tortoise, the Japanese fighters!
Good Bound-Face wrote "taxi" the hall December
Ladies'-club-youthful Frigidaire-men's-room red
Chanukah of a donated judge, to see
The Canadian pottery, "bee" was so characteristic-
Ally lacking in "these" persimmon-decorum of
Loud, that that. Oh many was the "hick of cancel worms!"
Her quiet wig was a parachute. Stones!
O the bad answers through a bin of petite ruins
Shines! "Magic. Earthface. Geranium. Bad-
En-Baden of pretty sharks, yo-yo-column, pin
Buying teas. O the mastery of his fenestrated
Shark!" Yo-yo said: "Die, Patty, of disease
Blossoming larger than 'we're'-tarts barking silt
Now in the midst of raspberry-time, which gophers' exile
Is merely a hack window, jumped down in the back
Love believing blouse, song cheery velveteen,
Mocking rose of gifting satin. Beds. Some
Deerparks." Day lifted their skeletons.
They came to the blossoming veteran; and fancied beer.

And terebinth, lobster of this season. Mudlark!
Oh, barriers were shooting, the billionth
Coffee of "wonderfully" dizzy tea. "Man, or
Cosmopolite, lair is the bird of mints'
Island. Balcony cosine of the hays." Each
Forgets to mention "that frozen candy." Birthday.
I am so happy that I could split
Fire engines, to know that blue is here.
I wonder if lobsters have always known how it felt
To care for the midway at most candy
Beer. Either, yes, tomorrow, is evil, or
I ain't feel it. There was "wonderful" chow
Last night. We barefoot the enemy. Glad
I have like her gold, yet glad
That, and serious tomorrows at silver toes
Free Island. O Danube! mirth, at
Tennis, was "the lea." They "danced" with me.
"I gladdened this worried Catholic bishop
Summer!" Daring Wotan, the King Lear of my
Courtship! For he is bringing "chairs" in the
House. His barrister walks: "Fading rose,
Mummer of the shy weird golden fingers',
Eighteen, a deserved aspirin. College
Is nice!" In that month, youth carried each frigate!

Monsters label his hill: "Mantle Hill, Cuckoo,
Air, Moth. Their gorgeous Philippines
Is friends of Ireland. Ask 'Herbert,' lowdy,
The weak cosmopolis of raspberry sherbet." Some
Time ago I forget about all proportion. These are
Crumbs. They dance. Its sleeping state. "Wonderful chow"!
O marriage with coastlines of aspirin. I taste
Them, "howdy, airplanes." This nice reason
Their chair hat my finger, is "don't," summer! Gee whiz
Of curtains, has lariat of she Fig Newtons'
Really. Ha ha. Are you hysterical,

Lefty, now? With what reason does your hat
Come out into the sleepy bottom
Up the Canada river, the merchandise, "Alf," dossier
Is late church. When last night we separated water;
And May-time habit clutched at tennis. These yes-
Whites! O odge, pyjamas! Marriage of recent white
With bear shooters, the Mississippi. Gin of cares,
Plower. O Jeep! red white and blue
Tans, rooming is Santa's first beach, class
Of beaten Gulf Gas, murders! Constant
Constant mad mad. Hen! engine of rejoicing gin!
There is a big airplane running O my
Blimp, across the defeated Mexicos of aspirin!

Daylight, now, this wreath of hogs.
Oh, there's a burglar called Smoky.
The bugle call is managed thunderware, the babes
In arms have all been turned to Octobers, with
Baskets in their shoes. I know this "are":
Baskets, murder, ending shoes. Each taxiing lobster
Knows that baby, she is as delicious as an orange
Blimp. Night! Tanager! O tuxedo
May conceited lobster! guarantee is orange
As "Molly's in the rowboat." Guarantee
Me the badness of each sharing strawberry
Of notes. She as taking out her under "Where
Are logs, cannibals, and sheep? Is this the
Malice, good summer! of a yo-yo's streetcar?"
Oh I lay on their bed, in the beginning, at the
Baseball. Carry me, Mary Ann, carry me!
You may think each hair is phonograph
But Canada of delighted wrong. Borrow you are
Blue. Blue out came to meet the bar
Flotsam gypsy earthwear reading, can
Of German blossoms, dentists in Cincinnati
Fancy attitudes, cotton to defeating summer.

"Nancy, Georgia is now quiet. Pale win-
Ter duck, meet limbo. May, hen, oh, Mississippi!

Military 'where are?' youthless, inks
Well 'git' mad, O sharp! Not 'over-where?' " and
Either youthless syrup. They man could buy
Location-qualify to "hees" lemons Jan lay on
Oyster melon charge account Epidauros. Match
Us, we, first inks: giant, cuckoo, and red, but
Maced gold, O sweetness of deceded chemistry
Marry. O the sweetness of braided celery on
Tile badgers, "he is the funeral of any cat.
O courts! March was 'hen' whist 'yew' ear
Funeral, cat." "In the mission house through Mondays'
Mission powders of marvelous pink (Death air death
In the Deathhouse) (Leap!) missionary
Cuckoo, loves, ape, mortuary, defeat, is almshouse
'Mary' House, we days of long
Thirst, cuckoo clocks sandy as green
Germany mouse Northrop. Ivy, win, you, say.
The America of—cocoa, ash, bin, ivy." "Nude,
Bandits, mouse, rosemary" "Wintry is the silence" "Marshmallows"
A. Lurid chances, stop. Fishing carefare.
"Indian bench malade. Wheat. Amble south
Is amble." "He wears the sweetest bench
Of bandits American is the world." Dancing
Of of. Oh! Loud, ant, the snow, waitress

Canceled the youth of day knee's blue waters'
Ceramic foster gun. Shabby
Animal crowding Hun. Bleeding knickers,
Perfect "came to alone balance of five weaknesses'
Sharecropping the crow-doughnuts of hay-peanut"
Jan lay, the sea had, when, comedy Epidauros
Weakness, "perfect," change for these marshmallows'
Contour, gee, simplicity, American yo-yos! sen-

Sens of peculiar mildness! The barrel is
An "country of embarrassment," to the charge un-dimes,
Not-waitress, enter the sea. You died of embarrassment
Winter, crazing pin of the marshmallows
Gone blue, magic at Easter; and the phones'
Welfare corset of genius again-society. "Nail me
To the pillow the Anna Dime of showering pillars
Severance mute alcohol." Major
Interest artist "Daniel" in the why be again
Their cots of snow O waist in the pink
Column! share of my east! savior
Of useless notes! Common way, the
Churches it aspirin, south un-day, blue manag-
Er charm that lakes to "Big Sea," un-Dane
This sleepiest one, dime land hokku kerchiefs
They. Green, the shirts of his table, lain down to be gory

Knees, un-, Lord, order, a, commanding Saracens
Carles li reis, nostre emperere magnes
O foolish Fords in Spain! *Set anz tuz pleins*
Tresqu'en la mer cunquist la tere altaigne
Bachelor, Hugo, and cockeyed Milton! win-
Ter arches, decency with eyebrows, gun-
Sight of brocaded fixtures, lockjaw in
"Youth Wins Each Private," lariat of mo-
Ronic; damp, who was your nurse? "My own." Stockings,
Whiskey, "Lay me. Bread limit that has tin sheep
Esteban Elsewhere, hoop! cold-blooded hymnal
Judge because the cuckoo leaps. Cockeyed mate
Wait till all "dear" Saracens "ant" in their tents.
Mix-up! Weevil-show-time! Hundreds
Of pages, holiday, tryout, fear, gold. Nan
Waxed "neat" to the Sarabandes, coma is Hans
Chalk. Pierre knocked on the cool weevil
For a British hour and a half as the nail files
Were old sixteen years old crucibles' marshmallow

Wheelbarrows' service yellow, O bonny balconies of
Hunk! Aegerian buildings mad in junk-
Red and the ponds of bell-ink coffee "of sweet true
Comedy, to say 'there,' " but Roland bleeds:
Pyrrhic, umbrella, my! hammock collars you. Cuss. Wheel.

Nine days to one you may the forest this
Europe qualify imaginary pastry notice
Summer hat curving to placard yellow
Dens of curving imaginary violets
To steep the order, "White illegal portholes,
Who dance is the sun, March wind, say Venice
In Sumeria, peculiar, loving potatoes, gone oyster
An, correspondence sweet, no out of blue
Andante, Shelley, these pastry follow
Their latest oyster. Can give each quiet blotter
So nude notice, end, tea, bareback rider,
All over town. Then sew, use the sea, mad
To begin where blotters the cigar-orator-
Hay-lobby. North anything off dream you've been
Ant, dear collies in yellow, barristers in green. These
Courses, wonder a white as no, be given, run
Who cranberries, yes, in backwoods blue
Till sigh, their challenge. Go, slim blockade,
Oats-dairy! We're not all back
Engining black, engines London, kiss, night,
Endow. Forthright is the sheeplike elbow
And the bins of a tern's resolution!" Weeping mixed
With "Golly, she alone kissed us!" and paper
Kenneths, thrown against the windows of outlifted airplanes!

Bay leaf! for you are burned by the midget sun. And
Marriage, to the cold, mint stables of anyone! Bay leaf!
Landslide! Marshmallow! Feces! Annoyance! Sew
These leopards into place. Bay leaf! Uncut faces!
Lumber! Wait! The curtain of the pyramids

Is lifting! Bay leaf! He is the pirate of underwear! And
She almost promises! The lark is their loosest hearts'
Greenhouse. They die when shirts. Some professor
Muter than Long Beach! O bad! dirty goods'
Limited sweet hearts! As now, she cereal-planes
Council chamber. Heatbox undie heart. O bound
Calico mirror of "ten sighs"! Certain
Nights I cannot sleep; the wind calls me, "Stewart,
Go out among the loganberries, preferably
Alone. The lake will lie there like a barber." I get
Up, and the stovepipe seems paler than Alaska!
Cold is the parachute, pea, fine the sun, merry
The purpling heart-commissioner, January,
Pencil, otter, Michigan. Orchestra beds!
I name you yet I know you, hopeless Jimmy!
What is the climate Monday pyramids
Bay leaf! etcetera. "Gonads have that clear pencil,"
She said; "the madmen have all retired. There
Is going to be April faster than next month when it's April!"

Showers, summer, handouts. Will the locusts
Be okay? Marjoram, chancellor of the pill creamery
Dollars you paid who to rest your house batty
Cemetery cloaca bended knee; evangel
Of the rosary batteries! What "perfect" yellows!
When Jimmy felt that orange chain he felt
The excitement of a parachute at sea! He linked
"Plaza" and "joyous parachutes." Nathan in his car
Honked. Uncle Parachute filled his camera
With joyous razor blades and "perfect cameras." Sleep
Walked carfare by the sea. A boat "pelvised"
Arcady, it was so green. "Oh, then,
Can't we marry velvet?" screamed Jimmy. Down went
The surf, in. Most often. He would have carried the yellows
Back into the cabinet of detective yellows. I bet
The rookies have never noticed anything. Sewn

In his car, loosely amid the raspberries. Shoe!
Lux soap might make you a swan. Surface, chimney,
Banjo. Hill, bicycle, aspen. Oh he shook socks
In wildness ridge, bounded off against his car,
Woke Nathan, fared through the wilderness of dogs
To surface, twined this bay leaf, and shunned airboats.
It would have been nice for you "that lemons"
Assume he is streetcars, O quiet half bench of wood.

Call, lean, boar. Swim. Is three
Birds. Win to. Sweet. Medallion-and-
Garage, tassel. Wheat. Lonely. Bag woods or
West-ear lemons. So, in no; and. Deep. Maharajahs.
Six. We will you us half lift is. "Oar-lemons
When" that movie is. Final. Aren't you liable
Touring-bee, us please? Shirt-India cars; and
"Either thou socks sue the sun, air-
Hole, tan surface, pear-clock, gemini
Ands youth, purpler. Thee, bears as pure sacked
Reason sunlight 'Mary' tellurium maharajah:
Blanqui. Their shirts water as
Mist! Who cold dassn't-Mary, theatre. Henry,
Soda Gun? Ouch, dancers!" Sunlight is those
Little with. In. Cow next door; rabbits
Year, fail-tent. Next coat. And January, theatre
Calcium calculo California ban, yearns
Calcium theatre, oh. Oh. Endance shoe
Mans. Un. Bare decent dachshund was, pour
"Ain't" trimmer wick. "Angel can wintry
Cocoas repair," oat quiets him, clan-
Destine shirts! Sandal of derring-do
Harangue by these fields Blanqui
Of Mary, and sunlights in bomb!—green, endocrines we next dove

Barricade "um!" dare Z horse in
Who yellow legs. Andes wrench news hand me the

Curtains win freeze: location as Chelsea blue
Finance tree, hook, deprivation. "He blankest of rugs'
Dens, toe, and 'character nearest bells-hills'-
Dogs. The soldiers wander him rum. Danai-
Cringe-yellows. Shaggy Ghents!" Now,
April hinges wonder parachute toilet brainbeat
Limerick surfaces lilac pessimism leaway merchants
Toys ant Jane you were's active neon so
Peanuts away the nominative air-green Indian
Momentous shall I peculiar lilacs button canary
Ocean billets man cloak Sumerian lilac orange
Lane banister sunrise Congo to sea
Bond mention sameness lilylike parachute. We
Foundation limousine the sea. Imagine that
Clothing! O beans, hinder climate red
Bandanas' come each oar para-seating doll-sweaters'
Coppering knee "Hippolitoid" "poiple" chaperones
Tree, songs ditch answers lemon. "Dear Phillips,"
Endymion quiet the merchant marine Saturday
Luna fan seed desk "Nursemaid ooh subway act dusk
Raspberry gee am cup ho-ho landslide
Mill, mano, risk, later" senators. Fenways, eagle and maids

Other "lingering" rabbits' youth lift fiery yellow
Nomination show-time assassin, "Sweet
Are my cares. My den is column, news,
Coliseum. Marriage are my bent
Gloves; and normalcy this Fenway muse as color
Sandy. Chow, and music's officer, see, hop
And dare musics' greatest lungs. Llama end
Hairpin balcony shoplifting color. Hi, blue
Bears! vote for me; I glow." Santa of So! O
Terebinth of teeny colors, an ocean's collars!
Mantelpiece! Unhonor quiet as the worm
Invents. Us, season of punjabs and death-
Mints' cogs, marriages with sheepdogs, beds, and

Stunts! Lintels, pow! are everywhere, care limns
Doped heads. Alcohol of frayed lintels! faro-
Delivery, O sleepy lungs' "placard" high, say, "Blue
Backs, General Win-Madison-Square-Garden April
Of querulous testicles!" Bench of the curving weight-
Lifters, solemnity of, hat, teething orange
Winter "May! hill!" sewily dear half nickel. And how
Pass chocolate, hens, pin day-suits, and water
Lariats! Soutine modesty China, ant! weightlifters
Balcony-minty. Canada, why: Easter say, "How stunty
Bear rose the, dean drums, 'an entirely fiendish wafer!' "

China there are benches on the chairdogs'
Color-wimple, "May I bent
These tedious ranches?" howl, Lulu! and I
Hairdogs' yes, I, when fine stooges am
A bare lea-snood, polish, rum, Andes, tiptop legs'
Mentioning gold dust to hay! Kinsey! Marxist College! "Ann"
Word! How! stables are we; end I yes
Dither; "she belongs to me fatter than a drugstore,"
Ben Jonson, shirtwaists, and pretty magazines'
Carolina, "Though mother is a new
Baby, Carolina, pigeons! Sherman for president! Molo-
Tov is diving tomb eye my tippy chaircar; lungs'
Dog airminds Atalanta's" Hill which first
I Monday Eskimo my inkbook; wheel hollow
Labor Alpine, this, dirty Angevine, sea, bear
Toy-poetry; "Make it a mistake
A your pyjamas, ace the. Lanterns on North
Can." "Youth Major servitude landslide
Cokes." Ha-ha the berry. Colors men. Inchings
Frogs and magazines. See at the cherry colors
Men, sun witty ham's cop rays, engine as
Sea, dogs. There they are, has, gold, in, hen.
Pardon me. Little matadors. Carcass's neat gold
College, he: yo-yo-terebinth, what little lungs!

America inch lover Santa cares ago
Bicycle; Me: Matchwrappers an ever rainthing ugly.
Wayne: Drag sheep away into maritime
Cupboards. Sarah: Mockery, colicky streetcar
Universe raspberry shirt pin lie sweaters'
Sweep, out, today youth over youth muttering, "Housetops'
'In movies'!" Are there lariats an defeating cans'
Choice rocky melancholy Jericho and-is-side pillow
Scene, seldom is Nevada, munificent, walk to cruelty
Angel. Eight art. Hoops pond links balance. Aaron: Mock
No. Otto: Gentle parmigiana, us key raindrops, crackling
Choochoo magician piano, red, balance. Lattice
Mirth—sandaled sheep. Ken: Doubled holiday, piano,
Miriam the mirror, Atlas, Liliom, Cambridge. What
Horses dune Marilyn key E sparkling? Hands
In cold as. Kent: Oar-shape, find the peary space
Mirth "hads" light at "time" the magician city
Nancy; truth masonite showers furniture. Anne
Endoplasm Cincinnati concert millionaire show
Their sweethearts every Ingres youth Jericho furniture, O
Canada, Havre knee nursemaid the tawdry wastebaskets is
Notepaper brassiere, O landslide
To "perfect" Greece! When I was totally, and "seize
Lemon," laudanum of preparing streetwalkers' sunrise clove-tan!

Scenic parachute. Column. Pear. Elevator
Sent hair swans. Bam the students. Pillow
Then Swedish underwear. Year-horse. Bogs
Season curfew than Atlantic merry Christmas howl
Inchings act students' dairy lazy us. Pegs!
Southern. O we "marshmallows" water its crazy-dairy-
Necessary students, interests yam then "Is some" shoe
Wait aw the scenic dairy in "Yes I am
'Tree' is 'melody spies' purple" oy their blues gen-
Uine great vanished cloud! Bins! clasp of the pre-
Liminaries too tinder pie rose, late, rosin, discovery
Banjo peanuts lyricism that rosin

Fails discover genius Mother's Day lank church
Of Country Pin! Banjelo, tangelo in
Meet— Hands! cloistered sharks! dairy
Farm of delayed face-dimmed "cosmopolitan
Asia fastest say wood Germany faculty defeated
Nuncio bled 'fanfaronade, gimp disky bees
Llama cow furnishing Delibes gamma raspberry
Jericho munificent function opera delphinium
Sheba!' " Axe! charity! kin-berries! lay-lows!
Opera bare your Chinese Polonius Ping-Pong
Slave Mycene Germany calendar reform
Savings bank endoplasm coconut sea hood foggy ankles

Easy to Coney Island, winter, and pep! O matcher
Of teasing matches, matador of "teethes," mangle-
Course of "seizing barricades," O colon, merit-
Eagle, bandager "Ozzy Carpet-Faces lilac mercy
Interest, ant, life," beaver, soon-you, bare
Agora in, moronic sukiyaki, O tenth
Summer! minus! Andes undie drifting shoe
Meritorium, sharethismatzo, end, Lulu
Born, scene, Canada, me, LeClos
Wolf! airwaves! sandwich, there are receding
Ox, maladive; merchant marine, selfless
"Solomon," fishes. Tarragon, Aragon, hula-newly
Endeared Ingres-shaped mint clods'
Jeer-storm-its heavenly mirrors, youthless ale! At
"Three Teeth." Amerigo! summer!
Bins! embarrassment! "Weir a cold half an angel
Den mid-altitude car reception decimation lie
Here, Z blue. Morrow angel Anza tune the
Morrow January-mirrored two!" Mentioned
Aspirin grin as lemons orange belt
Possibly do; chair coat midnight soap
Paris engine kimono eastern comma "their place
Tacit end alls you"-mate ear of, bat! summah west
Matchsticks Eden of is "Daniel" "urban hill!" Oy! Hail!

Yesterday an usual fainting pen bananas
Auto. Winter for my catching out flags not
Merry in my room! Denver! orbèd hags! O fan-
Shaped leaves' British Museum's stern
Aspidistra of brocaded Annamarie Lily Ann Ber-
Tha Leeway end America these day, O motto, modern
Ant fair impudent charm's gay beauty
Shellfishing doughnut-ankle's arm Mildred
Lois, and these, iceman, the tear-men, E
Soon, wave me, modern, blue-ascendance Cal-
Ifornia, day, mantle, sorrow, lands "Lindy
Maritime hunch knee baloney youth he's French!" I
Nearly fell auto this museum! Lair-bins,
O comicals! Majesty, their green and suitable hogs'
Ten guitars which mother I climate
Sun grateful Marie-banister-soup craving their blue
Deer, the men who cocoa lilac
Hips of peace January mistral hemp Detroit
Of saving lurid nits, O mouth, curseway to the south
Might-Helen, syllabic (bet-chair) gin-telephone
Louder than the earthware thinks! "Charles? Telephone.
Teeny, sure to send Dale a sundial."
Central are the token seas. Tender Labrador of bees,
Paper antonyms. O the hill picks up, that is pink.

Weaver, the bandanakerchief, a hen's, nuts'
Shannon. Looms that take care of America! O
British guns in Glencannon! Palace of gloomy
Insincere physicians! Moron of every positions
Heaven is cutting the passive mirror too
Close to us! O Rembrandt in a bottle, sleeves
Of the joyous pituitary, maritime
Interests, coalescing "Mammy Slope-the-
Pink-up-into-them-," believers in wattles!
O bear cats! bear rugs! bundles of Shinto wristwatches!
Goateed shoe boxes! lariats of striated dust! mints

In comma formation, San Salvadors, mirrors in
Transition, senators, cosines, and nuts'
"Chair which he might dance balance blaze
Knee"! Oh! Ocean! demon of the dem-
Demonstrations, the sweet formations, wheat-hap-
Py neat-fornications, O savage! licorice as
Broadway! What number in my shoe! Faro! Lie
Down! Shave! Miracle! Borax in Neptember, flock-
Magine, genius-blessing, toss! cure-you! They
Are not mine! O anono, a May "thyme," a "nuss"!
Bravely I built you at Faro, jail-word-
Sin-ban-chill-sane-pollen-car saying, "Tweet
Ins!" Motionless air raid! bungalow of peaked clay!

No wonder! parachuting germ hay-mow squad and king
Every ant is king! minnesingers in gown-
Boxes, ladies, money; WE
Childhood sew, weak ladder peppermint Balkans
Every mild is king! banjos (aye) going
"Yessirree-streptococcus," Mercedes
Avenue, win D shy parachute of the oyster
In enamel youth plod hinge parachute
Down hair, motto! Boled parallelo-
Grams, weaver is not king! Jaded, though
Mild ands ant, blotter, yo-yo ship sate Jericho believer
Angevine "Sewn in his car,
Loosely, amid the raspberries,"—hokku! revolver!
"Winter comes among him, latest coffee
Peep, oil, April; Angevine, cop, noodle,
Hinge, birthday, Peter Pan: 'Say it is not so
That why bee weevil dinner landslide mite
Caretaker, blessing his handkerchief; whereupon
Laurel and Hardy.' " Certainly tomorrow is weapon
Pleonasm. Dancing, like kosher ice water
Lays. Rob the conceited strawberry, engine
Count on the deceitful oyster. Imagine the

Sea, that knights! Borrowed his fading isinglass
Ankles, cocktail shakers, churchgoing leaps, umpire, Virginia,

Biltmore, "Sue Group," matches, all go, "And
When we had almost turned to aspirin, the
Paris of three-feet germs," O notice-
S of green and limpid lemons to "an
Office, air-built, nine offer," Mary-chute sen
Sen battery milkshake oh are hottestblue
Lends, and weewee were to be seen (badger
Nexus of youth weed anvil-surly borax! Shah!)
Tour, acey rink, momma, YOU
Came, dancing whippet of tie-college, hoop! yo-yos!
Bather, banister, sleepy sight, ant, mutts'
Quietness needling "are hoop chair" is
Encephalon, oyster, the weariness crying
Encephalon! matador of potassium phalanges, slim
Hobo, militant cheesecake, my real
Merchant of Venice, The Winter's Tale, Two
Gentlemen of Verona, Salome, labor of the defeated images
Or-Kenneth-strous baby for "magic location, thou
Lazy Boston in aspirin, sweetheart, earthway piano
En-soma lemons." Ore-parachutes! better than the Island Queen
As sting sighs, O mint, church, sail, Sun-
Day, whoops, in rocky Pittsburgh, sharpening pencils
Beside the leafy badger, notice how
Bare arms singing "Wheelbarrow," merchant marine, cry it. Lemons.

Ornithology, man "hid"s in glass! whoppers
Of Dean "A yes joke," rum deceiving by
Hay cooked balcony swart lemons in. O
Columbus! Can doing beery silver naturally "wheem"
Georgia of costing Sea Arabic,—outlines
More "entire empire" sweet asterisk yellow knee
Khan rabbit. Sofa, peanut, end girlhood, how
Lorgnette de-orange all, in white. Orchards

Of dental sonnets. Add ad ad. Hand orchestras
Hay-knee "ousand Meary Thousand"—Yale
Okay acorn is in in-orchestrous phalanges'
Podge! More! the caretaker is free with aspirin
Showplace America to-me; cost-Max! O backs
Wonderful, eagle angry's-light end, O! arrest
Oyster. We, after all, more pink bee, solder
Airy banner sea toy carpets, baseball
With hand seas; O wagons! Shave the
Lea angry ope behind orange "Lag, up from new
In, as, woe Jericho this difference wonder," acts
Silly; worried whom green-O lakest badger,
Nouns! Winter, Caribbean, curvy elope-grange-
Masthead: pigs! "Science tells me that you
Are a pig"; writer of handmade orchestras,
Bather, "end," willow a, church, fin, aid-fool's

Sigh photo dream cargo sit loop worm, hike! San-
Ta S weeping pigeons oar gore ninetieth
Working bended bow is "nineteen," axe our
"O mustard-wanton" streetcars O shyest red
Eight and April imaginings culver Lulu silver
Banana peanut savannah. Hollow buildings
Of "Die now, mother No-forks lethal
Ale-blue silver," color, moth, ah inch January
Flag-pinned; shy savannah-green forks "egg"!
O not! Bearing chute of dressed tomato's
Yoohoo coastline opera-eagles, jangle
Odd. Oyster favor disintegrating marriages
Table yellow, "Oh summer is hot for fools!"
There were British linens in the
Tepee emotion disintegration glamour garage
Nonsense magazine olive midnight cuckoo
Gyroscope titivate America gingery showplace
Shallow lime wit motion Santayana O cuckoos,
Grey, fearful, yum yum, happy, our gypsy pow-pow

Mayor, sty of distasted elephant-elevator
O shiver prunes, nightways, tea-deserved sob,
"Am I losing this mantle of scientific lemons
To Hobbes?" Idiot, ankle, bakery jobs
Kisses, and migraine gobs of *Hamlet*, a China of sentences.

Formed by the note-taking of mud-pushers, as
Formidable as violets. O fair field of the
Form of Hussars' climate of conceding harps'
Fork jujube aimless Louisiana, O wraps'
Forest of "Lee Herman jail." Salivate in
Focus, nineteen ninety oh sunshine, back
French, livable, dairy, engine, choir-man, sea
How fair are airy strawberries' feeble
Monster anguish, oil! Oop-Oop the Janitor! Fire
"Summer," his contentious "lane." O sorrow-waiter
Of mines, and "Wifes of cotton! butter! water!
I am crazy in the lintel of your cups'
Parachute Madonnas! O misery of samples. Sea!
Marriage gee umbrella grapefruit, houses
Of rotationless cars' marrying season ere
Yew, O glassy oyster of deceiving green
Anciently Pyrrhic lousy able to
Junction pool incinerator theatre badgers,
Badgers, badgers. Eye! winter! goatee!
France! O culmination of the side step, Peru!"
Angel answer "den step" "con-feeble" orchard-motion O loops
Of "Wow, ethers of cream cheese!" De-
Grelotte the chive: "Ignorant summer madhouse,
Douce working Madonna—lilac, cuckoo, disintegrate!"

Oh there was a bear of ginger bugs! They lo-
Cated ox, ink-millionaire, duck-balcony, O Jan-
Uary the blimp of oyster-Pisa! Shine us, nicks
The pear-coop balcony. O coptic frogs! See
"That," silver ceilings, olives, Cho-Cho-San

Of smiling truck. O Bridget! Junky! Hackwork!
Sleepy-come tables, lustrous pouter, he, gin the
Lake opera satisfaction deserted hankies. "Yes I
Comma serum baloney cancer shoe
Buckle China deserted lemonade, for you
Of all youths. Bad luck! blue! Indians'
Safety devises, O grandmother Forest! Links! Foremen
Without shoes! Lilacs gigantize my my my
Earthest lilac lie lye delinquent, shoe, wax
Joking, about-miracles, gentle, able, goo-goo, golf!
Lime insurance! O barricade of loft miracles
In tune with: grills, pier-accountants, gnats, gorillas,
Morris dancing, spies, peas, llamas, and chairs filled with gorillas
Last night: Georgia of pleonastic squirrels'
Frigidaire! toy bloodhounds! O bough
Of crusade lanterns, how I love you!" I bit,
With my "ornithologeeth" mackerel hum baby, cuckoo
Copley Georgia dimple yo-yo Sheba
Networks. Act graceful, blue! "Day and here nitwits."

Shirt "and vivacious quiet feels you"
Barracuda up "Gee, knob" they (are)
Cow-fables in genius Gloucester. "Ye
Arch noodles," grapefruits
Give "fair" boscage to needly Rockport. O bands!
Roman's! lintels! steeples! sagas! bands
Of (white glue of day, earth, Japanese winter
Under mile-an-hour kimono, whee!) shoeshine
Marriage of (shabby industries ape big south
Of boobs) lime ginger ale of lilacs (Poe
Jealousied fruitation bounds Andes coo rig
"Dynamee" poop deck "sun-marine" un-"Go, lazy jasmine"
Bike, water; happy boat nit, is as oh ooh ump
Ape lala newish, 'ray! Jewish Shasta
Of brocaded bumps, minerals with lifesavers'
"Attachable-andiverous-ology-lulu-cars" buying

"Yessy" space, orchards' changing mirrors, and eye
Of deceasingly grouped lemons. Look, jobs! So
Mary Janice silvery palace Edgar Poe
Fin giant, boat, chase, America; aorta of
Nixing lemon jobs. Waverly! and councils of jest-
Chalk, proving by entrance, oop giant palaces,
Lint) ha! to winter (shorter pear, then very blue,
Express-leaves, answerable) or bee, red yellow.

(Shower paybill ocean pin-bear agora Lulu
Gin-pear ice of gripes loganberries with sea
For Latin names archway and oyster polly
Knee fandancer peaceful showplace O blobs
Of paradise shining like sill-pill
In Orient Romany shining selling successful
And eagle bathroom night-Orient oak-cow and
Airplane of shirtwaisted barristers each
Mildly okaying solidity to boulders dam and
Advantageous going to sleep butlers louse
Hay nook contingent planetary
Inventory nunnery, harbor! O wax, "vax"!
Postulates of deceiving acid gramophones
Ixtapalapa yo-yo January naked cripple
Of telluric lemons O bond salesman
Streaming with held rugs bindery
Of paraded oh-ohs, eighteen me that
Lindbergh slumbering mailman-osis piracy luncheon at
Packhorse, giant trade unions Mayed, dove,
Gramercy thoughtless Lindbergh, O keyboards
Better than the city's navel, Shostakovich
Of drunken caps, "Gee Vizzikers," to
Town we heard them say, "Sizzle go fizzle bandana
O Santa, lay down the coping saw!" Boats! Good night, tea!

Commuter, joy, rabbit, air "even"
Khan dairy-shy "wheel" give me,

Stair ink dove. Pants of Rome. Rake
Bannisters of bee, star, fate mink pans
Georgia each terebinth agora, Thousand
Listen. Maldoror weewee hoop baby. Oblong
Sen sens. Leaf-brick. Hoping
Bay-sea pier-attitude are "glove"-pink
Shorthand nylon air-pilgrims to bin-dove
Noonal phlegms, achings badger rake! Ore
Din of hope lea "gas" mention shy
As in Shasta, dabble—cornice, mandrake
Seraphim. Oops! "Quiet be my double. North
Bandana cuckoo indentation hoop we; air is
Ulster wanter, a Jericho. O bills! And neigh
To me, janissarry, pilgrim dividing snow
Manges, town me shay sea dirt devising rains
Doughnut on high! Octember of the jeeping bear-
Mackerel, sunder! Inch of teas, peas, and pink
Layettes, O morn-a-phones! Jane! Jane!"
Dippy weave bay deem housey "erf!"
Giants, "ipes" remember Oberts Plossom
Gingerwearing tea fenestral stripes
Choochoo against against. Act is, matinee!

Ozone, ips, dismaying humps! Lockwater
Of gingerwear manteau! for I pierced
Bicycles, Manuel de Falla. George Ozone
Fell bike dead Hannah-master the shoe-ox,
Blips! Oh, Cajun, inch; house of the starry itch,
Master, jujube of beep-beep eagle classicism
Horary. "Light me hoo-hoo chaste
Agora delicious eagle bumpkin sobstory. Edge
Of the beebee adze. Germany shouts, Hello,
Baby, than-hortatory!' Orange midnight, cous-
Cous an 'border silly' yum yo-yo I
Plate ooh dada atch aitch itch eye knees higher
Than as is Wabash Wabash checkers-pyjamas."

Orchestras dimpled that month, climate!
O backbreak of the fig-poker, tablet mirror
Cool gin-jujube. Borrowing heck of the Stars'
Is-manifestos' Clarissa of coo-neck. Pie, die
I, bun, oak, love-way lemons breeze altar
Hip weary clove. "Mention the shopping parachute
To Billy Cathay, shaving about India
Quiet yes halva shoe-department geranium
China. Jonah models paregoric." Plagiarism
Of sunny stars! massacres of the little models
For "Bee, Arthur, talent-way loops ginger adopt where you."

And once again her stomach functions normally—
O parachutes and zeppelins, good morning!
He sassy fawns, we rally; ope, ope this
And mandarin Jill, hoop the girlish beach, loss
Quiet in, in, dinner function: "How
Alabama the finch, chair Otto us decency crumbs
Dinette happy normally. O good morrow,
Finch." Amos, the plaza leaped
Abnormally incinerator good mood. Water edge
Engines idea in lemon paper; he shoves
The water away; it is "their." A long
Wrist, Jeep monkey and "locust for good
Location, rioting red raspberries hove
To Alps of comic gin—Weight! mirrors! as
Phonograph as decency abnormalcy banana
Joyous screen penumbra group wait ah
Pill! Oh, how did you get here! Weave
The curvacious zeppelin." Mary
Me O now it knocks. Plaza? "Gypsy." Earliest as
The weekend of focally month lemons
Happy. Shy, shy, shy! Fiend, fiend, fiend! O arid
Lams, goof, pier of brocaded nuts! Fishering
The lamented dish, is a sofa, A. Goof,
"Dish-a" air, airy grandmother "soofa," "bahg"

Nymphs of Boston! Caruso of the pilly chafing dish!
Periods of pink, pyjamas, we: a noted weariness
America illness pyjamas; cow food, lemons
And gypsy raspberries! Oyster, Havana, the common sense
We olive eagle perforation choir gypsy
Sweetheart. And the tennis scones. Cow-raving
Island bad, mad, "oopal," shoes. Hay
The simian as day, bay, dermatologist
Eleanor, "she-food was dully sheep-food
Only as ear, waving pyjamas," grandmother
Of the screaming links! "Out! Up! Ear!"
Basement, "tea-pool," Ernestine jujube coliseum
"Arf-woofs"! Lady, cloak eve banana wool
Might eerie and "arf-woofs." Idle pin!
Wary Indes, speech of grandmother, or
Ore, ad, Dillinger as dim rotation agonies
Policy germ, taffeta, ink's cuticle. But his
"His" is "Is"; as is baseballs of weary fizz-
Lyre protector,—orchid of cow-faced pyjama-
Career-waving shove-malady on Cuckoo-hay
Links, bobs—of hit mirrors in yo-yo hare
Pursued leafy suitors. Oswald Mobile Bay
Easy blasphemous giant "is" root beer casket
Under gal Chinese wastebaskets,—O brilliance!

How serious was serum, and the wave's "apric" therapy
Tonsilitis-ing cocoa-dandruff to soothe Labor Day
The Menshevik chilblains toot-toot gypsy lemons'
Cloak past you, evilly riding that bicycle
Rain, shops and. Houses of cruising furniture O dots,
And dandy, manned cuckoo by quitter-labels
Of shy-announce, April-beer, common-cuss, ware
Blue gypsy, O nincompoops, daisy, Aristotle!
Weary is the merchandising South Pole. Orchestra kale
Is near. "Genius of clowning and cussing bananas
Of daily 'blue' and seep, joy, joy sleep of teary

Purple, the Japanese movement of art stars'
Bangor of shipping 'can-knee?'s! Owl-orchestra
Of the shy dandy music shops' distinct
Diamond Avenue horse-porpoise flirtation, O beans
Of 'sody'-metropolis's weird-wee gigantic-blains
Of bundler-nurse! Oak buildings
And shy lanthorns, pilot of graves' damp horns
That chirrup, 'orchestreed' pill-more,
Unshabbiness! O loophole than loophole 'thass'
Eagle of silent bingo, groups! Bessarabia! this
Distinctly! apples!" Very nutly they shine
"Beaver" "Clue" "Pylon" "Imp" "Kentucky" and "Biltmore"
But of orange greens, lane violent raspberries.

She showed me his or her nurse, O ices!
No kiss or railroad station as bitter orchestras
Basing loop quiet tarragon-way-pats of blond
Madonna. O jinx of the shyest sphinx's
Axe-flotation career-numbers of backroom
Tinny notices' limbs of collusive
Plug-its-planets, opal! dime is dancing! And bakers
Follow his wilting literature. Actions!
Pins work, "follow" his sweepy limeade. O
Now-monsters! April castles is Falernian
Jowl, big lintel of teeny January
Bug railroad-station bicycles, bug! hi, bug!
Gypsy, bug, and "Am, yo-yo, blue, a bug,"
Cycles, orphan, often, a bug, "Yay, oh yes, a
Bug," hey! hey! Isn't ear a walk
Down wavy "ladder-somes," or passenger
Climates, white! red! Carolina! ancient bug
And a mottoed sail, dear faint aster orange
Monthly duple say quick-sail-as-unbottoms-
The aster rouge, in the closings
Of every literature. O continents of buttons
Where are we hiding? From? Ooop? Alpine bug,

"Gingeah," history, lilacs true little fiend
Of tyrant limns, bologna! This is that.

Dairy of true green bugs! "At all," eye
Weird conclusion orangey pink hammock whistle
China basing fair, elephant, tie-
Hanger, "it's music of the spillwort
Fooling 'Dumbness' Castle, O climates of the
Waving and catatonic arms of pantries of
Blooming ink of pantries of."
Pineapple donation cuckoo interrupted me:
"Shoe, house, bitterness, careless in shop
And gonad farm, what learned detective
Of colored submarines, quiet Dixieland
Of these shamrocks of blue, embarrassment of
Eating two cups when only one was
Served, the delayed parking meters under a lake
Of lion-parachutes, O collarbone that wins
The fairness test, gin, and cover for the furnace
Of kings' sighs, January, Easter, the bent climate
Of culver, leaf listings, O! tan!" Shy
Rain, and the beauty of the "dug-
Out mirror of that steery Mexico: class
Of blue air white unconscious, sea
Pasting in harassing loops of green
Dichotomy to 'hoo hoo' funnies." It cleansed
Uganda. One series of crazy gowns.

At all! at all! pink metal, and
Beer-crazy medal of keen "has his worst summer"
Ice junctions! "Tomorrow ivy Gogol jewelry,"
Hairy, true sea, landing phone, oyster, bag
Of disky rockets weeps away, hay!
Rackets is "timpistuous rizzberries," icings of love
To care some,—"inginns of timpistuous barracuties'
A-vailable injinns." O April of the terrified revolvers

Aiming their women at the shoe boxes
Of my hope! Legal, faraway, cokey-mutt forests
Of the limitless jail, him, Ann, in and
Is Andes-knees! cool, cool is rather bombastic
Or cuckoo deep-sea forests honey-monastic
Oh shine wherever! and the Georgias of classical honey
Country hoop! fizzle! majority limit
India-cakes-is-revolvers-cancer! "Tie paper giants
Hop yo-yo Norse ring. 'Eep' sheeps
Time Andes bassoon ever gracefully. The red where
The final oop! oop! of granite ginger motorcars
Of quite green. Cow, that my neighbors are sleep,
Ginger, parade, hoop, May." Ah! linden, where
Evil Edith eaten the enunciations of
Tea, thunder, and the bare parachute edge
Of "Lark, hoop-walker, teapot-they-go to" sleep!

Now it is May in the ape. O acids
Ceremonies of artificial end as so autorides! duchess
Bees Santy Gloria of "Do nice," broken addenda
Of "Hoping today piracy automobile
Idjit dampness, O bag! this dampness
Alacrity of the automobile" "For waving flags
O an incinerated bug" "Bag!" "Andes, why not win
'Her' " ale and now Waverly do so
Basement "Al Lemons": cot where eye believe
Panegyric sweepstakes custodian day-
Brought lyricism to these cuspidors. He wakes
At night, looking for the shadow-boxing
Cousins, April and armistice; but mystery
Enshrouds the answer and deep regeneration
Forest to the limping funnies, and blue
Is her daylight's agrarian following; for she
Lycanthropy-odalanalyzes the tippy rainboxes
At jesting match-drops; since weary ovals
Most happen here these climate of some days

I walk. Terrified, shire of bear-
And-cotta sodas, he ginger-deers the
South, a light, for mirror of some days; equal now
To a deep ship, Ferrara, flags—swearing,
"Bonny Asian sacerdotal dove,"

He leaps pinstripe flotsam balloon cab's
Killing people wintry, eep! loop! simplicity!
Anguish! "O Andes of a paper dove,
And little miracles of my simplicity
With painful aspirin and smiley railroad dove
Of 'sinsuality,' see the minute that April dove
Me, birthless, hoops, lilac, and closets, iron
Saviors. They gave an orchestra of milk
To the ships and their first grape dove
Ships. For weeping psychoanalysis! and paper beds!
O crossroads of silvery paper, how
Jericho and we nifty whiteness I bled
Superior wardrobes into the railroad: a dove
Of China's paper, shyness, and a wafery head. Which
Lincoln of the surface bananas! O pots
In Havana!" "He leaves me have a banner like a
Grapefruit." Shorthand! These islands are a pinprick
In the sea. And yet. "O cameo, O bope, obe opeep
My cherished Solomons!" Feenamint porphyry candy
The bed was soft. "And yet I left there
Like a silent weir, bonging the clavicle
Of 'meelions' of tea-barefoot frogs; or their lanterns.
Oscar, simple, silly, city, ocean be-
Hind 'Prologue to the Canterbury Tales,' in bed!"

Mouldy apples, quiet limericist, hay! hay! dove!
"Dunciad I flailing food awake.
O barracuda uprising sleep snake sweet
Cow nifty hurrah surprising dawn, itching *Iliad*!
Cinching banjo! Jinx pituitary rosemary

O grandfruit! jeepy in the lilac nursery blessed
Betweeny 'gold-foo' and 'hooray-lips' nursey,
Chancing upon this Aragon 'injinns'
Slime to leap awake mercy! Papery!
Oh how the orchardy ocean lilts! Ape! Perfidy!
I fought him. I gate his head. Nigel Green
Said, 'Bees are without mercy.' I
Then said, 'A bee may not be without mercy
In the lilac future category of curtains
Which fail like tins made of lime.' She awoke
To the summer. A blue ass bit her knee.
She turned her two salacious eyes upward
Toward monotheism. 'I am scraping the
Halibut.' 'Are you a Christian?' 'No.' 'Then
Why, why are you aiding and abetting this fish
To be the summer?' O passionate oysters
Of November horoscope, unmarried hair
Of the morning sea! This mourning is beyond me,
The land's light upon sin's ornate weirdness!

Toe, its bench, we lay down in Illinois,
Anxious pilgrims. O loops! How the sea made war
On its arid tramps—of ginger; but nowhere
Cobblestone mirror garage blue two sea
January and 'Meet the finch': lilac! actress!
O melted kinship, in April, lariat of the two
Trees, blossom that is attracted where
The hill suffers, and motions softly downward
(Beavers at lunch, and biers, this is jasmine
Of smiling tomatoes) go toward, and after
Sombrero, oh cast a the lazy and into wear
Out isle 'in smiling silk' janitors
Of tea-tea'd warfare, surface shirts, cot
And bear, O bays bees cuckoos as free
Everywhere! Cart him away. The eaves
Are as freezing with leaves; and the sky

Of love limericks loomy coastlines at Garbage
Point. Or are there other shamrocks?" In tin
Sales why oh air Wyatt nut linen unusual
Ha ha ape one times destiny. Leafs cockatoo lemons
Piece of. "Andes dam de-bear, hay! hut! sheer!
They say that Mirabeau went nuts in Sweden
Behind the shoe-filled sea, yet at Amalfi
Balanced (oh ho ho) a green pill on his saber!"

April of belonging merely to his blouse,
She yelps. Oy! Beans! the sea! Badger
Noticed us yippee sat down in his chair
Simply cemetery. "Each whiz!" Powerful flights
In sea willow ouch orchard ankle
Of drooping beagle; and then! ale ale-letter
"Zimplossitude." Ant, a "shrimp of coruscation he"
O air deep-kneed checkers in a Humber
Of Turkish sighs! Pans me the hare
Of "economics," O linens linens linens!
"There are very factories angry sea,"
Ankle doughnut behind too I dream "ink-
Parachute-whiskbr" oom! oh I nigh no dimple creation
Different lassitude. "Tea-jamas!" Mirror-boat! A dance
Begins to sea. O lariat! patiences that we seize
Margins in into our weird fights. Bag
Of enemies! there are limping morons near your boat. Let
No bun stir! And the antlike idiots were
There, eagle, matchstick, an inch, and the fairground
Of due nickels; latch; wins. Oar "cattle" coming off and
There bee were opp oop oop! W. C. Fields in
Tosca, the billboards, a cow facing a mop
With these words, "Top hat in the underground,
Booby!" Han! I she hails, the nicknacks of acid.

"In my loafers I went to jail to see my brother
Perish in his little loafers beside the iron fountain

The milkman refers to yesterday as the Electric
Chair. I forgot, however, to bring along my blotter; and
When the electric men began to slug my brother
With tan shoes they had, on I mirrored Oscar Winter
Yo-yo tell them, but asterisk! Ocean of near 'misery'!
Hint that I was saying he sits in the chair
Near a water, of ladies' faces; and, oh, pyjamas
Lifted unto my hindsight their ladder-lantern. He says,
'Don't tell them back at home which I miss
Them,' and, Lord, I most to half empire gymnasium tears
Maggot; but loverly I bonged the hackwork cigarette
To novel inch as civilian lemons. And when, Monday,
Or someday, I am flying near the
Baseball of leaping electric lemons! For pottery
Is my shoe. Now, which I wish to say, and
Good! is this I don't care, for the modern childhood
By the sea which your Noah's Ark promised me, and I say
'Blah' to their mint stables of jugular whiskey
And veins of green talcum! I want to whoosh
Down an armchair, inch of the summer sunlight,
And find my brother, the grayed one, still reading his newspaper
And using his toothbrush, *or* using his toothbrush. Goodbye!"

Porches of dismayed patchwork how goodbye
This summer sun is! and these novels, cockatoos
Like the banshee umpire, thatself, wimple remarked
"Coop, ork, new-chestra, tin, gingeah, India where
India is suppose to be." "Now I see the nylon sunrise
Coming up on Whim-Bole Bend. Anna lays her matchstick undies
To the sweet finger, to the sweet finger of the wind. Bare
Roommates choir where lady seabirds ank-
Le comma weary dollar. Ape, but he makes money!" A
Garden momentarily films George Montgomery and
Ina Claire, monosyllabic, clue of the red ragweeds.
Oh now I know you! ape, red, panic-car, Kismet
Of diseased, ant, hill, roadhouses, school-pigeon

Of the tippy as rainwater motorcar! Clark Gable and Ginger
Rogers fall beneath the wheels of this motorcar
Of cheeping staff officers. How the gray leaves chirp
At the stereocopter filled with flying
Character-studies limited only by the harp
With which they publish "Myrna Loy, a Grapefruit of My Lilies,"
In quarto, and with volumes of lollipops, to document
Everything! And the green robins chirrup
At the sun which fills the dominant
Sad cars with its bilge; and the lofty ladies
Who limp through the bottom of ponds, singing "Raise us!"

"O rainwater how hairless you are! and when winter
Accomplishes everything you are as mercenary as gin
Today, deceiving the pilots of enemy airplane
Is loophole, ant-lake, and churchy-wise. Eye,
Simple doughnut apartment remember
When sunny a sandy daisy ripping in the country
March winter labor delicious party in my eyes;
Green whirlpools laughed on my foolproof shins
And I clambered through an Airedale 'win-pyjamas'; he
Told him I they warranty métier. Show
Of a creeping bunch. Of limitless lilacs; and where
Are the goldenrods of Schenectady? Near you. In Orpheum,
Giant 'theayter,' O lake-country! Where are the beavers
Who sought you in wanting clothing, parachutes
And 'arid climates,' and one, day fought you with
A bacchic soda of genuine airs of piers? O pod! park
Of the rotationless beggars nearing coffee grounds
With their airs. Airy hairs. Little minute. 'Injinn.' Cigarette.
Barefeet I waited ere the barracuda
Bared its air-sweet tinder-bet of rain-settered
Air-confessioning, 'a thousand and one minutes!
O rainwater how hairless you are! The lands of business
And the weirdest summer, oh!' " Lady in comic pyjamas'
Lacerated sleeping foot's bicycle of Limping Classics!

Mirth-marshes! how often a baked fly
Has fell from the swimming goldenrod of a clip
Notching the youthful daisy
Magazine, and lotioned you till its daddy,
Some mockless cheerleader from Syracuse,
Has fell. He fell into your jeweled eye and found it!
How marvelous is baked caddy! Remember the swimmers
Who raggedly swore by that film about "Eagles"? O mocha,
Years is so dense! Ankle compare ginger-rod
Notation dense. The year on its weeds of fence
Angel, thou, mirthless as the blackbird. It's somewhere!
And the ankle basement trees causeway sanitation
Lyrically matters to, has been, and so, Samara,
Jay and Sarah, gypsy goldenrods! O mottoes, mottoes, tomorrow
Is famous! "I live here. I buy my gasoline
Around the corner. And so I want to ship
Three liveries and a half of giant clematis
To Norway, in heat-bill dancing jewelry. To find,
Tunbelly fish of romance—sand page of blond Indians. Who
Sleeps in the nowhere of fire-basket? Somewhere
That's an institute, and the records play
'Climbing through Montmartre as balloons,'
And no rugged apes play with the thrushes
Who hand them sliced baloney until, married, they play cards."

Now she knows I notice everything that she notices,
Even Hawaii, so she has stopped placing notices
Under her sweater! Banners! And ingots
Of the lightest lots placed nearest the sewers
Of her choice of my mottoes, and nearly
Has fainted, I boxed magistrate seamstress demons
Who ride into hot shops! O calcium in deserted rococo
Spades! winter wear! "Why for me
In binges another, candy, thus world of brown
Key if dust, motto of the care-foot sleeping and deserted
Cranky rickshaw, in which he placed his lemons

Overnight, saying, 'Leave these here until the morning
Boldface type singles. England railroad expands
Feet.' Face and the roaring doctor mountain
Each England campfire carfare doctor, hurrah
Lake-strips. Penny. O commander." Clark tubes' shack May means
Going a lemon from home, ah gingerwear! these horses
Plaza geranium eep-temptation. I know! They face
Klotch florist's tomorrow, and bingo! how lethal
Are short faces! yes! "We lie, people, in deserted bags
Around the harpoon of his tipsy poetry, the
'Beg' that whale nought 'leg' yo be contented. Marseilles
And October in the sailboats, cook are near." O hands! Cossacks in
Desperation France-ing his sybarite grape hoop-cats!

O whale of girls, burgooning
Late. Oh! my "knee is fair. There I limp
Weevils into the air," Roger, whip
The decayed easels, "And plenty
Horseradish, it is airpower, accident insurance,
Tea of papers, and rowdy lemons. White Pomona
Of the shrinking star-cuffs!" "We! Ay
Annoy north and building. Latent
Pyrrhus!" Hey Jane! Log cabin wake up whoop
Parachute tin peanut lake. "Air of a
Million, shine high upon, dreary lemon. Loom
Of pare, all niece, the flower of
Accident insurance rag boats and leaves engines
Pan, April—uncle-weary to ginger. But, oui!
Clothing, sing-worms, and fail! my joyous gasoline
And caney stars, O spillwort!" Ape. Ate. Ben-
Seeds was late, oop! he went to high school
In a, ork! yes a blimp, oh married to the knees
Of not having, Indian as sharks, the reefed money
To order O doughnut coconuts there, weird
As mated, alcohol, the "ginger," a synco-
Pation, "Anagrams! fish! pools! babe! hospital

Of the careful linguist-itch-hand-fields-youthful-
Kentucky!" Evenings, places, a, it is a

Romance! under fields! one sorghum powder keg
Of chafey golflinks marry to barracuda
Left-wing childhood Santa Claus pyramid lilac
Birthplace changing Eskimo! Snuffing those pears
"Lately I advanced hats Eskimo. O tears
Of my First Wild Wheel, a laboring thatchery
Of sea-high, grouped cuffs! navel
Of the business laboratory, day an orchid's
Way birth cardinal season-animals
Went beer fear notification jailbird machinery
Of bees like 'gone' whim 'flam' oh inter-'mooped'
Pathetic lucky badger sea! Meant Wormwood sea
Of E double interlocutress's silk stockings
Making never seem like yesterday! Oh hop
How been in the!" "Jane. Hoop moorishness an ridge
On lilac cubbies." "Orange orange am-I dimple,
Immersed the whole sea?" Joke! Wish! Paintbrushes, toe,
Alabaster! "Onto which grotto and a sea-brush lemons
Chair-face gin-ear-all's matting time and Inca of
Careful soda shutting chair-faces oyster shooting
Dane-way of mirrors loons ant, 'arf-woof'
Of British gleeb, the 'nembus' of 'son-away'
Curfews' and naily kerchiefs of demon curlews'
Map-opping 'para-kiffs' grandmother. Is hen."

Oh yes, the golf balls! "We were three golf balls
Yesterday until pilgrim milkman rhododendron
Pansy of navy gorilla, limpid shoe box
Ten mirrors away. O lake, rape! these
Are the bedroom of furnitures own
Aspirin these are the daffodil aspirin the
Daisy desert a microphone of golf balls
A 'micraphone,' a big nimbus, a hoop with daisy

Rarefying the mixed-up Popeye air, oh save me
From 'Cuckoo aspirin, Margaret the hell is
Tin impy, lie! banana." O Lou
Air! jadey was the cindery gym. Manners
Did not save me British
Aspirin and lips lion tiger daisy O meres
Auto: "London I gave you daisy auto London;
Hit the believed sissy! Magistrate
And dippy 'legistrate,' Camargo
Silver ferris, 'lasp' the bundling wheel
Of silvery golf-bells." May! paper-ladder!
Sincerity! O basements of childish loans
To gangsters "eighteen century mint car" diz-
Zy lamp under it shoe fine Ken stars weep
Cemeteries bee "uselist" snow. Corpse-Alps'-
Zither maiden, see, "Tamarisk the ocean!"

Serenade the minting ocean! jump
"Bee" lilac fishes, oh, football, shortcomings'
Now on pink sand boat O
White goat, staircase, "Santy's eyes
Amid them blooming group," solvency
Barracuda, ape, shortcomings, Bloomsbury
Of a sheep's copper knickers, O mome,
Tin of raining sen-sens, no, no, no
More waves of petting football
Air-condition, solidarity. He weaves
A necklace for the sun-dry
Of masonite sewer-mind a beach of lilacs
Meditating weevils' cherries or "ots" miling
The silvery cave, the victory of lariats
Over knitting! Bandanas! "Opera programs
Lead me. Listen. The field lay there
Lilac shoe. Mistinguette's Schopenhauer's
Coolest, very, bugs! O bony tops
Of the scarab, chairs filled with rooming houses

In the 'mine are very idly act gunflower
Serum ladies.' Soon they will bear those boats
A wave, nexus." And the mere light
Health lateness is boxers O cam in "flodge"
Of the tear "Kish" sea, man or ear is weak.

And, as, they. Oy lifting the bear
Opera India sweet net, where gin time
Soothes field a hay-coop of missing cherries
Arthur closet balancing "ictionary" the true
Blackboard in's blossom, daiquiris of blue knives
Rompers as "dinner ware," the deceiving licorice
Clientele. Milkmen! Salesgirls! Strindberg
Of crazy ocean! bell thou
Lane—equal—box hats dance uppery
Sum the Alps, O may tent soap box
Seeds! Factories of knitted daisies'
Cold semper fidelis, cheesecake, billboard, a matchbox
In brief case, as, lazily for the beard that
Beard that beard. Oranges and earth-lazy cherries'
Seen cups, oh or all. And. Nina Castelli amid the
Sweeping shrubbery. "Bankrupt soma, how chaircar
The will is, are they hills, toe, serious,
Loma, April, orange, serenade. I listened to Tchaikovsky
Where cows of pink. O nickels! the breadline
Of sleeping chills, thou merchandise
Leaf, in the lilies, of a hairline, this, 'commentates'
A dear savannah, the belts of alone sake
Reeves ale up toward walk for me, O Guinevere
That untie somas, of a nary work. Oh do green ships!"

And Alaska. Is, as, but. O Samos, blue! Near
Ships dairy mural dairy ships. Lantern ships
An daisy hue, might some are green. Nina! April
Soho kneeways. Barracuda of shining "Mexican"
Strawberries, liberalism! O aged green darlings

Of the 'Mericas, hunch, zippy! O location, look
At the merry, donning, palmettos, fairways
Of that biffing colossus "Peep Peep"! O
Doe! Marriage in Mexico amid the missing lemons
Of a parachute shining into the Mirabeau
Of your tasty kiss up in the March stars! Socking
The papery mirrors the limpid summers the very sutures
Of a timely stars' nimbus! watercress, O bough
Airy middle of giant impure true parasol swimmers
Blue. Toy-nature! In the bilges of a fair
Sure audience! They played "April Tiger," "Dig
Please," and "Secret Anatomies, a Parachute with Lemons
April Breathe Look Who Is Summer." Pickpock-
Ets and a different season the bridge us myster-
Ious lollipops' gambit Toussaint lurid seagreen bananas'
Shapeless crony, in the pyramid that all is
Life or purple! O gems! and beers
Drank up to the knees our green car baseball
On cheeriest red. Porch, thimble, and steeple!

O paints if time! A bough. Drinks the cow.
Unfaded red lemons, Santa Claus, marine, ow
Passenger, a London of musical coastline
"Sarah-fuge," benches gone equaling wavy "nice"
Halls. Save the defeating bells! Bend
My mind's six loops! Ah, beavers in the hall
With a trireme, merry coconut Triton
In, fall! the parodies of cinch, a stream
In Denmark, a basin of cherished spools, limping
Lanes, of "When, Mary Ann, eyes lakes is India
Merchant porch summer lethal leafy swim 'white
Rebus among dare homes is blue' is air wombat is
Is is is," banshee caretaker, suture, green. Ho, conduits
Of the wavy breast-line, which cylinders
Hat youthful climate! merry-cross, of "beads"
Of "beads" of beads! O bear! Hand-silly melons,

Believer-wear! Shoe, shoe, shoe! I dare you
To limp along O the fair mountains of a lifty pansy
Air rift! the bugles show. I dare you to
Mints, oh is golden! the bear-shaped leaf-cow of buy
One-two-tree-pony, of "never sees one blue page chair"
Harpoon limerick O the bee-parrot, "the werewolf
In the newspaper paints an orchestra" so
Many merry autobahns, boxing spinster!

O meetings! with gold bargains angel blockhouses
And bins, uppy "care-loose" seed! Weak nameplates
Umpiring the seaworthy Southerner-
Lake-opera, the killed mason of a dairy stone. Line
Meads! O bear the deflected milkmen, hog, away!
In the bishoprics of lime. "I am pasting silver
On Dad's picture. Ernestine
Lies in the garden, imagining the linemen
Galloping toward her silver pastry. I am alone
In my belief that Sheba leaks. O sybilline
Cogwheels, Saturday! Dreams you are the lantern
As the is foetus's punch." O daisies win! "Whin
Warren walked in Warren Warren's warren
There was limmons on the sea boat rail. O pail
Of apples that give the bargain clues
To its leafy gold! Pin-binge!" Lusting a meadow the curtains
Sail fifth shirt rail, "O bikes' last
Touch, now musical cancer!" Sheeps the hog away. May
Down, its, there, icks, tunes, "Solve me this some where
Blue cradles with their puppies, and the tinnest light
Of the 'worrild,' a manager sun green and surprise
The lariat of speaking hogs." His life was red, but
Oh, hats hip "Lear" of day. "Now-tation"
Of the singing rifles, which share, "zebras."

Maids! oh, a Moscow motion picture
"Flimmed Alpine blue," genius of mothers' crass producers'
Flayed livelihood of screeching juice divided

Into mysteries, boat, lilac professors, to the
Lemon of knowledge, bean, bean, Atlantic
Ann, "Miss Historical Peach Tree of Nineteen Forty-Three
Orchestra Idiots Nineteen Fifty-Three O Green
April of Vanished Bananas." Shirts! made in pylon
"Chimeney" manufacturings' damned blue
Sheep-castles of deluded carfare, weaving nudge,
Weaving nudge, O bombs! Loops of lacy match-
Sticks' blossoms' faint head's child's weak last
Cry's hoop-tiny May-ville poop deck's "as
Langerhans musical bayou of sleepy lemons' shy
Rare shy rare's act's" act's axe! "If need
Be peach! Blossoms of merry showmanship in Stone-
Henge, bugles! Loops of "the caretakers' jangling cigar's
Loops' rung-demanding caretaker's sweetpea's
Pylons, amid the clamor of rug-maddened seats'
Paper of closest-knit words' blossoming rugs' fair
Blue railroad eagle nine-tenths then will look out the
Windiest rose of fair harp-maddened space's lifts-up's-
Sky which nominative sea's solo cinch-
Lousy-mats' tree-church's a billion edge-nursery!

"Anna, soda their brains." "Father, finish is certain." O basements
Of cardex, "muneeciple" rungs'
Badger, agent, elephants that silver money
Career number "is" most, and try to die
Annoy "the Badge," lawn there wind from at seat
Lives is-maybe acts, who, rose, love fell
"His aspirin." April of we moss
Whos, Andy us where wind maze opera's we
Golf links, say "Egbert. The Floating of
Hips Blossom. A Nightmare of Amorous Delays. Thought
Turns Green. In What Century Mazda As Famous
Pericles!" We is running through his
This rowboat "axe" everywhere a fashion is factory
Celery leaping rose, agua. Hatred! Parry
Chute O summer of green "Penmanship is

April's pants," lovers amid these penmanship
Iron stars and latest can't-we-go-hosiery-of-the
Face British lilies! O bough
Eep-ad baby "sooma" and junction thousand
Lists May sweet "cars a a a a pill, season
Clouds of in and O emollients care, foot, blue
Evils," panzer. "O Kenneth tea Arab baby easels
Felt *arrondissement* gypsy tables and limps of
Needles parachute peas by, Lincoln, accidents."

He, day, believes is dogs "ne'ertheless" a
By the fishes' cocoa of today's sea sent
Collar loneliness home babies papers labors
Neighbors eagles capons savers of lilied
Papers of carbon moose's ape-bottling wintry
Soma of "a rustic Jeeps" facility, dim-witted men
Lying intercarfare raspberry "cup, be aware"-artillery
Amidst ye someday raspberries O Gloucester
Of faded robbers, cattle-bakeries and lint
Phosphorous eateries, mags! "Wearily woke up
Green bowwow. Artillery." Shapeless militarists
Caped Bongo Brow. O gypsum
Penthouses sweeter than a rabbit's pillows
Of airy green "Knocks," bakery
Of distinguished sighs! "How came the locks
Lethal paper incinerator vicinity choochoo fractions
Cuckoo nuts paper Freilichers if lilac sea-bottlery
Towel dispensary?" There air is very weird
Ape bit summer green air care "poop deck O lovely
Poop deck!" Black cherubs "a" shins
Lesson. Boat. Backseats motion its
Yellow carry us. Din to the "stair" of teeth
Blue mezzo soprano of sweetest decay "Indians
Air, blood, out," as bee-axed crazy-bell wigs.

Weevils, him! A Sue Artillery. Angel. Lye
Dim apricot, comma common comma. Change.

Priest-ape. Bay-foot is and
Laxa-team en-merchandise hope Savannah nearly
Congo. And bounce! Labour Party football lovely
Air "right bread to dam is must we limpid
China fateballs." O pennies! rime
Shirting a, sea: clock, to bridge—at's lovely
Sick's is wall easy as lovely dam-flowers
Lay America easel bunch! Hate! Equal. Lions. "Hey,"
Is the fields' operatic major amnesty smearing Congo
Silver "bear." Lives. Bicycles
Limerick the shorty beach O cosmos
Of "Last winter," tower of pin-hitting
Lambs!" Maid! Tree Hoop! Three "hoopers'
Ladies' night foot out tear inch above children to
Shirts. Bin. O lovely green
Aspirin. A limps. We." Ham expostulates
Swimming the bells. Tree-punt! O music of the
Shamrocks' peanut amidst the doughnut
License plates the ear silk. "Putt
The sob!" Nara of "Lame, I boat." Meek. Lilies'
Paper milkmen-tie. Us! Pills! O Labrador-
Peach-quiet mittens' tea sun of cleared ozone trees!

Majesty O a blue arf kneeling hoop
Satire "Peaches need, owl, off, woof, May-
Time, 'the sea' of embarrassed fresh asphalt
Pastry laughers Lincoln of believed
Santa misty sentence nice clam deer Eskimo green
Solid. Rooms!" if sublime "grapefruit each-terrace
Lamp mice cooling-system licorice bizarre labors
For distance mighting silver coaties of green
Lay appearance proffers death lilacs nigh
Air gum in the 'shoot southern!' of prance 'kra!' knee
Sabotage 'limities' of shooting 'barbycuties' malice
Tots' visit love poultry sea bashing huts in green
Agoraphobe, O pain, Stevenson, Washington! Ship,
Mummy, woof, barefoot, lobster. Suds of air-

Proof. Tin. Bee-license. O reachest of the bays'
Spearmint copper 'neximo' axe livelier is toys
As engine-Britains, leaf, an miss. Sew, eep! the sun"
Bells asking lyricism is-mop. Corpse! Uncle
Pins! "He is sweet to" imagine
Of tree highest lint nuts hooray substitute
Fair limb a fields as cigarettes. Shy
Bessarabia puzzler eagle by "We waste" cincture fezzed
Clouds of preachy lakewater altars eep bell
You-you clubs arrive, Gemini of the hat ear eye fall peach water

Deem rafter. Cemetery. "Leem" eel batty bone.
O boa. Of the Fez Theatre. Laps'
Tricycle of we motionless London of bees'
Pent lilies and hooray schoolhouses'
Musical today loop lantern is surprise "schoolhouses" '
Peanuts' ladies' aspirin lanterns
Of climbing clematis, a lake of conceived doves' "Go
Fine ear character waiter. Modern, lilies. Congo
Of the defeated railroads, revolver. Lacy coat of the
Chancellor's ink mirrors of. Insane celery." Ship.
"O bayou, boom, icicles sesame the contained robber
Of leaves in chairs, savanna!" Crane? oh heron! Able
Balance the trip knee, comedy. "In the heap
Of Maytime llamas I limped upon the knees of
An old charcoal. Lemons" for a pound of the
Oxford! September air! Bun of old leaves of
Care each musical "Hooray, unpin the gong," sylvan water
Ape shell-ladder! Egypts! Mezzanine of deciding cuffs'
Anagrams who tea-tray "sigh them" objects "pay-sign"
"Leaf-boat" "love-object" "base-ball" "land-slide"
"Tea-ball" "orchestra" "lethal bench." Sum, are, lakes
"May-nagers" "love-times," sweet
Counter ale pan-banned gypsy-bin fools cabana
Gentle hiatus of sarabande "roof" "wide" seam!

Notes

The Chase—First Day. This poem was inspired by the chase for the white whale in *Moby Dick.*

Highway Barns, the Children of the Road. "Barns" in the title is, of course, to be read also as "bairns."

Ellie Campaigns After a Candidate's Defeat. Ellie goes on campaigning even after Adlai Stevenson's defeat in the presidential race of 1952. "Elecampane" is a sweet-meat and stimulant sometimes referred to in pre-Elizabethan plays.

Poem "Sweethearts from abroad." The "locale" of this poem is the Cedar Bar on a winter night in 1953.

Pericles. This play was inspired by a John Cage concert downtown, I think at the Cooper Union, at which the conductor decided to repeat Cage's piece (which was full of silences).

Guinevere, or the Death of the Kangaroo. The subtitle is a sort of echo of Hemingway's *Death in the Afternoon.* The Weisser Elefant is from Rilke's poem about the merry-go-round. The Mexican and animal-killing ambience of the work was the result of a short trip I made to Mexico while writing *When the Sun Tries to Go On.*

Where Am I Kenneth? Janice in this poem is my first wife, and Frank is Frank O'Hara; "Lambeth" is probably there because the dance "The Lambeth Walk" was popular at the time.

No Job at Sarah Lawrence. In 1953 I was looking for a teaching job. This poem was written in response to my failing to get one at Sarah Lawrence.

The Kinkaid Subway. The poem seems at least partly about the power of having one's own private subway.

Your Fun Is a Snob. The scene is a friend (the painter Jane Freilicher) standing next to a cigarette machine on Third Avenue on a winter day.

The Man. I didn't exactly write this as a play—there are no stage directions—though I can imagine it as one. I was intrigued by the idea of each of the parts of a person having its say—in the case of the heart, a rather long one.

When the Sun Tries to Go On. This poem was written in three happy, somewhat anxious months on Perry Street in New York City. I wrote every day for at least an hour or two. One probably invisible influence on the poem was *War and Peace,* which I had just read. I was fascinated by Tolstoy's way of seemingly including everything imaginable.

A NOTE ABOUT THE AUTHOR

Kenneth Koch published many volumes of poetry, most recently *A Possible World, New Addresses,* and *Straits.* His short plays, many of them produced off- and off-off-Broadway, are collected in *The Gold Standard: A Book of Plays* and *One Thousand Avant-Garde Plays.* He also wrote several books about poetry, including *Wishes, Lies, and Dreams; Rose, Where Did You Get That Red?*; and *Making Your Own Days: The Pleasures of Reading and Writing Poetry.* He was a winner of the Bollingen Prize (1995), the Bobbitt Library of Congress Poetry Prize (1996), a finalist for the National Book Award (2000), and winner of the first annual Phi Beta Kappa Award for Poetry (2001). Kenneth Koch lived in New York City with his wife, Karen, and taught at Columbia University. He died in July 2002.

A NOTE ON THE TYPE

This book was set in Janson, a typeface long thought to have been
made by the Dutchman Anton Janson, who was a practicing type-
founder in Leipzig during the years 1668–1687. However, it has
been conclusively demonstrated that these types are actually the
work of Nicholas Kis (1650–1702), a Hungarian, who most proba-
bly learned his trade from the master Dutch typefounder Dirk
Voskens. The type is an excellent example of the influential and
sturdy Dutch types that prevailed in England up to the time William
Caslon (1692–1766) developed his own incomparable designs from
them.

Composed by
Creative Graphics, Inc.
Allentown, Pennsylvania

Printed and bound by
United Book Press, Inc.
Baltimore, Maryland

Designed by
Soonyoung Kwon